The VALUES-DRIVEN Family:
Second Edition

Marc and Cynthia Carrier

Values Driven®

"The Values-Driven Family: Second Edition" by Marc and Cynthia Carrier

Copyright © 2009 by Marc and Cynthia Carrier. All rights reserved.

No part of this publication may be reproduced, stored in a retrieval system or transmitted in any way by any means, electronic, mechanical, photocopy, recording or otherwise without the prior permission of the author except as provided by USA copyright law. E-book printing permitted for personal use.

Published by Values-Driven®
(www.valuesdrivenpublishing.com)

Unless marked otherwise, quotations are taken from the Holy Bible, New International Version ®, Copyright © 1973, 1978, 1984 by International Bible Society. Used by permission of Zondervan Publishing House. All rights reserved.

Scripture quotations marked "AMP" are taken from The Amplified Bible, Old Testament, Copyright © 1965, 1987 by the Zondervan Corporation and The Amplified New Testament, Copyright © 1958, 1987 by The Lockman Foundation. Used by permission. All rights reserved.

Scripture quotations marked "KJV" are taken from the Holy Bible, King James Version, Cambridge, 1769.

Scripture quotations marked "NKJV" are taken from The New King James Version / Thomas Nelson Publishers, Nashville: Thomas Nelson Publishers. Copyright © 1982. Used by permission. All rights reserved.

Scripture quotations marked "NLT" are taken from the Holy Bible, New Living Translation, Copyright © 1996. Used by permission of Tyndale House Publishers, Inc. All rights reserved.

Scripture quotations marked "MSG" are taken from The Message, Copyright © 1993, 1994, 1995, 1996, 2000, 2001, 2002. Used by permission of NavPress Publishing Group.

ISBN: 9780981972015

Values-Driven® is a registered trademark by Marc Carrier. All rights reserved.

Table of Contents

PART ONE: The Journey to Family Success 7
- CHAPTER 1: ENJOY THE JOURNEY 9
- CHAPTER 2: WHO'S IN THE DRIVER'S SEAT? 15
- CHAPTER 3: THE COMPASS THAT GUIDES US 21
- CHAPTER 4: ARE WE THERE YET? 25
- CHAPTER 5: "MOM, I'M HUNGRY!" 29
- CHAPTER 6: THE JOURNEY BEGINS 33

PART TWO: The Parenting Part of the Journey 35
- CHAPTER 7: POINTING OUR KIDS IN THE RIGHT DIRECTION: *TRAINING* 37
- CHAPTER 8: STAYING ON A STRAIGHT PATH: *ENCOURAGEMENT* 47
- CHAPTER 9: THE INEVITABLE BUMPS IN THE ROAD: *DISCIPLINE* 55

PART THREE: Defining the Compass Points 65
- CHAPTER 10: FROM START TO FINISH BY *FAITH* 67
- CHAPTER 11: WE'RE REALLY *NOT* IN THE DRIVER'S SEAT: *SURRENDER* 73
- CHAPTER 12: FUEL FOR THE JOURNEY: *LOVE* 79
- CHAPTER 13: BEING A DEPENDABLE VEHICLE: *FAITHFULNESS* 85
- CHAPTER 14: *WISDOM* IS SUPREME 91
- CHAPTER 15: FINISHING WELL: THE NECESSITY OF *SELF-CONTROL* 95
- CHAPTER 16: WALKING IN HIS STEPS: *RIGHTEOUSNESS* 101
- CHAPTER 17: STAYING ON THE STRAIGHT AND NARROW: *HOLINESS* 105
- CHAPTER 18: HE MUST BECOME GREATER: *HUMILITY* 109
- CHAPTER 19: THE REWARDS OF OUR LABOR: *DILIGENCE* 115
- CHAPTER 20: YOU CAN'T OUT-GIVE GOD: *GENEROSITY* 119
- CHAPTER 21: KEEPING OUR FOCUS: *PRAISE* 125

PART FOUR: Parenting on Purpose 131
- CHAPTER 22: MANAGING THE FAMILY PROJECT: *AN INTRODUCTION* 133
- CHAPTER 23: PLANNING IN PARENTHOOD: *DEFINING THE SCOPE* 135
- CHAPTER 24: THE NUTS-AND-BOLTS OF PLANNING: *SCHEDULES* 139
- CHAPTER 25: THE DREADED "B" WORD: *BUDGET!* 153
- CHAPTER 26: RISK MANAGEMENT 159
- CHAPTER 27: FROM PLANNING TO EXECUTION: *TEAM BUILDING* 169
- CHAPTER 28: ARRIVING AT THE DESTINATION: *CLOSURE* 179
- CHAPTER 29: THE JOURNEY BEGINS 183

PREFACE

The Values-Driven Family: A Proactive Plan for Successful Biblical Parenting was originally published in 2006. At that time, we had just had our fifth child. In our parenting journey up to that point, we had read many books—maybe too many, because integrating the process of parenting with daily living was becoming a bit confusing and even seemed overwhelming at times.

So we went back to God's Word. Marc undertook a thorough cover-to-cover study of the Scriptures and we began to see more and more not just what God wanted us to "do" as parents, but how He wanted us (and our children) to *be*. Essentially, we discovered that our goal is to maintain close relationships with each other as we also grew in fellowship with God and allow the Holy Spirit to help us mature in Christ-like character.

Granted, the goal seems a bit broad and there are many ways of accomplishing it; however, we've learned a lot along the way that has been of practical help as God has worked in the spiritual realm. What we have tried to do for you, our fellow sojourners, is to put the pieces of the parenting puzzle together into a comprehensive package, so that you can see not only the "big picture" of where you're going, but also successfully meet the smaller challenges of every day.

This revised version is not substantially different from the original. The authority behind *The Values-Driven Family* has always been God's Word—and that is unchanging. It is some minutiae of the practical things, and how we have implemented different systems, that has evolved along with our growing family and these are the slight changes that are included in this reprint. We hope that you and your family will be greatly blessed along your journey together in the Lord. Thank you for sharing in it with us!

Blessings,

Marc and Cindy Carrier
March 2009

PART ONE: The Journey to Family Success

"I gave orders for all of us to fast and humble ourselves before our God. We prayed that he would give us a safe journey and protect us, our children, and our goods as we traveled." (Ezra 8:21, NLT)

The Values-Driven Family, Second Edition: one of many books to choose from—why did *you* choose it? You work hard and love your family; you certainly want the best for your family and are doing all you can. But there's something that's driving you to dig deeper.

If that's the case, you've hit upon something that can change your family forever. Be forewarned, however, that this is not just a book. If utilized to its fullest potential, it will become a lifestyle and a journey. The destination is family success, health and well-being, and in getting there you can experience a level of peace and joy that you may not have thought possible. All of this is achieved, ultimately, by cooperating with God's plan for your family.

Chapter 1: Enjoy the Journey

We have not yet arrived at our destination. In fact, the journey to family success is one that we are traveling along with you. We'll be perfectly honest—we have no platform and no professional credibility. What we have is a desire to raise our children well, and the desire to enjoy the life that God has given us as we do it.

We are average people in just about every way. We are college-educated, but don't have advanced degrees. We live in a modest home in suburbia. We drive newer cars, but not new cars. We have six children, a dog, and a couple of cats. Dad has always worked your typical office job and Mom stays home with the children. We are active in our local church and want to do our best at this "family" thing because we love Jesus and want our children to grow up loving him, too.

Even before we had our first baby, we had talked about the importance of family to us both, and about what it would take to do it "right." We were committed to living biblically—living by God's Word and teaching our children to do the same. Yet even when our first children were still very young, we experienced the typical frustrations. Not that we expected life to be perfect, but we *did* expect that if our hearts were right and we were doing our best, we'd experience a lot more happiness and that things would be *good*.

And therein lay the problem. Things *were* good. People said we were *good* parents. As our children grew, we received many compliments about what *good* kids we had. Marc's career was blessed and he was recognized for his work ethic and his management skills. Everyone who came to our home felt welcome and always commented on how well kept things were. So, with all this going for us, why did we feel like there was just "something" missing?

Quite simply, we had it *good*. But we knew that there was more. God had something *better* for us; and in fact, we decided that we didn't want to settle for anything less than God's *best*. And that didn't just mean being good parents.

After reading many well-selected parenting books, and taking away something positive from each one, we've arrived at a rather surprising conclusion: every book on our shelf focuses on our goal as parents, which is *successfully raising our children*. For us as Christians, that means, first and foremost, that our children embrace our lifestyle of faith and carry it into their adulthood. There are many ways of doing this, and we've read our share of the theories.

Through much of what we've read, however, we've been encouraged to measure our family success by externals. Unfortunately, with so much focus and attention applied to "symptoms" (like the behaviors of children), we've found insufficient emphasis given to the primary influencers of the household—the parents. An unfortunate outcome is that parenting becomes not only child-centric, but disjointed from the rest of life.

The Values-Driven Family was written to provide a different perspective on parenting—one that can make life simpler, not more complicated. You will notice as you read this book that the focus is more on you, as parents, than on your children. That's because you, as parents, are the driving force of your family. If you want your children to mature into responsible and loving adults, you must be one yourself. *You* need to be committed to living out any of the character traits you wish to see your children express.

Another difference between this book and many other resources is that we don't just want to emphasize the goal of parenting, which is successfully raising our children. When this is the case, we're either explicitly or implicitly encouraged to put our own selves, as parents, aside, in pursuit of this prize. No sacrifice is too great if we end up "winning" in the end.

Problem is, we don't know if we "win" or not for at least 18 years. In the meantime, there are daily frustrations and struggles and sometimes it seems like we're putting everything on hold for something that isn't guaranteed. Although it is selfish to think, *what about me?*—let's face it, we all do. We don't just want to labor and strive for tomorrow, but we want to experience God's blessings *today*. Family success is a journey; yet not only do we want to arrive at our destination (successfully rearing our children) but we also want to *enjoy the journey*. The good news is, God wants that for us, too!

Other family-help books may provide you with a map that tells you how to get to your destination; however, they don't help you enjoy the ride. These types of resources, which may represent worldly parenting philosophies or "expert" theories, are like *Mapquest* or *Yahoo!* Maps: they look like they'll get you where you want to go, but on the ground you'll hit dead-ends, unexpected road closures, or detours. There's no substitute for the guidance you get from the man at the gas station—when you *finally* give in to frustration and stop to ask for directions. This guy tells you, from first-hand experience, how to get back on track and ultimately arrive at your destination. He may not have a name you remember (like Rand McNally or National Geographic), but he has the goods to get you where you're going,

Part One: The Journey to Family Success

and you won't be frustrated by all the roadblocks that the big guys don't see. We consider ourselves one of those gas station attendants.

We've exhaustively studied the Bible to see for ourselves what God's Word has to say about how to "do" family. As we've faithfully lived out these precepts, to the best of our ability, we've also implemented different systems that help us accomplish the overarching goal of successfully emancipating our children—that is, transitioning them from *our* authority to *God's* authority—moving them from *rules* to *relationship*. We have experienced day-to-day peace, joy and success that we would not have thought possible just a few short years ago.

Yes, we still experience frustration. We still wonder, *are these kids ever going to get it?* But, when we feel overwhelmed or feel like we're missing out on God's best, we've found that it's not because of the method—it's because of the delivery. It's because we're not doing things the way God wants us to be doing them, or exhibiting the Christ-like character that is his goal for us. As we seek him and his ways more and more, however, we can measure our progress and feel God's pleasure.

One of the greatest truths we've learned and lived so far in the journey is this: *seeking God's direction* is *perfection*. In Philippians 3:14-15a (KJV), the apostle Paul writes, "I press toward the mark for the prize of the high calling of God in Christ Jesus. Let us therefore, *as many as be perfect,* be thus minded." Note the italics added for emphasis—Paul is saying we are *perfect* (or complete) as long as we are *pressing on* in our calling! This is a great encouragement for any parent. Although we have moments where we'd like to give up, God doesn't give up on us. He also doesn't expect perfection. He just wants our best efforts; and when we give it *our* best, ultimately he blesses us with *his* best.

This book is our attempt to take the whole of Scripture and apply it to everyday family life, so that not only will our children leave our care serving the Lord, but we will *all* enjoy the journey. We'll be sharing some of the amazing truths God has shown us, the practical ways we've applied his Word to our family life, and the good things that have come from bringing our lives more and more in alignment with his perfect design. We pray that you will commit to joining us on this great journey and experiencing all of the wonderful blessings that God has in store for your family as you live for him.

The Elements of "The Journey"

Early on in our Christian life, God showed us the importance of living by his Word. *His Word is true*, and with that being the case, we'd have to do our best to live according to it, make decisions based on it, and measure worldly opinions in light of it. We're convinced that because we made that commitment, God has been faithful to show us his way, bless our efforts, and give us abundant grace when we've fallen short of the ideal. Indeed, the Scriptures confirm this; Luke 11:28 tells us, "blessed...are those who hear the word of God and obey it." The "blessed" life comes from doing it God's way, to the best of our abilities.

Because we have made this commitment to him and to his Word, God has been able to guide us, step by step, to greater and greater family success and fulfillment. The metaphor of "the journey" helps us see how the different elements of the biblical model for family come together.

Imagine that you're getting in your car to go on a long trip—maybe traveling across the country. If you want to get where you're going with minimal stress, it is wise to begin with a road map and mark the roads you expect to travel. In life, the Bible is our road map.

Before going on a long trip, we also determine who will be doing the driving, how we're going to measure our progress, what vehicle we will drive, and what we will need to bring with us on the way. Likewise, on the family journey, we are wise to address the fundamental elements of *leadership, values, discipline,* and *stewardship*—before we even leave the driveway. If our journey is taking us toward family success, addressing these essential elements ensures that we'll make the trip with minimal conflict, stress, and difficulty.

Applying this analogy, the navigator of the car is the family leader—other family members are simply passengers; the values we live by are a compass that assures us we're going in the right direction as we attempt to follow the mapped route; the vehicle itself is the discipline that is required to persevere in the journey; and stewardship is the fuel and supplies that we stock up and apportion over the course of our travels.

If, as a family, we're on a journey, then what is our ultimate destination? Most will say it is the Kingdom of God or even fulfilling the Great Commission. Our everyday experience, however, reveals that there are additional responsibilities that must equally be addressed within the context of family. The apostle Paul affirms this when he says that the married man is "concerned about the affairs of this world—how to please his wife—his interests are divided" (1 Corinthians 7:32). Indeed, our family responsibilities include working, parenting, maintaining our marriages, and even resting. Yet we should *also* be committed to serving God's Kingdom purposes. All of these things, together, will constitute God's *purposes* for the family.

One of the unique responsibilities for parents is that they are tasked with serving God's Kingdom themselves, and *also* equipping their children to do the same. This is a unique call to discipleship that demands a long-range vision. The key to accomplishing this complex goal is *balance*. Balancing life's demands, living by God's precepts, while maintaining focus on God's purposes, enables us, as parents, to live out God's purposes for our own lives *and* effectively help our children to grow in Christ-like character. With this foundation, they will be more likely to willingly embrace our lifestyle of faith and fulfill God's purposes for *their* lives as they grow to maturity.

REFLECTIONS

Questions:
1. What types of parenting resources have you explored in the past, and how have these met (or failed to meet) your expectations?
2. What prompted you to purchase this book, and how do you expect it will be different from others you have read?

For Further Study:
The New Living Translation (NLT) of the Bible tells us in Ephesians 1:5 that God's "unchanging plan has always been to adopt us into his own family by bringing us to himself through Jesus Christ. And this gave him great pleasure." God has a heart for the family, because it has been his desire from eternity to make us a family in Christ. Our spiritual family brings God pleasure! Did God design our family lives to bring *us* pleasure as well? Using a concordance or other Bible reference materials, study how God has made us Christians a family. Think about how this model is similar to our earthly families, or how it might be different.

Chapter 2: Who's in the Driver's Seat?

On our family journey, *leadership* is one of the important elements that we are wise to address before we even start the car. Biblically, family leadership is a father's responsibility. Dad is in the driver's seat on the journey to family success.

Joshua was the leader of the nation of Israel and also the leader of his own family. A mighty servant of God, he exhorted the nation of Israel to "...choose for yourselves this day whom you will serve." As the decision-maker for his family, he then stated, "as for me and my household, we will serve the LORD" (Joshua 24:15). This decision is as relevant today as it was in ancient history. God calls us, as Christian fathers and family leaders, to choose to serve him wholeheartedly.

Unfortunately, the time-honored, biblical design for the family has become increasingly skewed as society has changed over time. Today, the role of childrearing is more often seen as a mother's responsibility. To be sure, mothers *are* uniquely suited to bearing and nurturing children; it is for this reason that God designed the marriage relationship. However, women were given as "helpers" rather than leaders within the family unit (see Genesis 2:18, Genesis 2:20-24). While mothers have a *role* in raising children, it is fathers who bear the *responsibility*. Ladies, that's the good news! The news you may not want to hear is that with responsibility comes *authority* (Genesis 3:16).

Generally speaking, it is unfair to hold someone accountable for things over which they have no control. Therefore, since husbands are given *responsibility* for the family, they are also granted the *authority* to make decisions as to how the family will be provided for, educated, governed, and the like. A wife's role, then, is as God said: to help and support her husband in his endeavors. After all, he has an awesome responsibility that he can't manage alone.

God gave Adam the task of working the garden of Eden, but said that it was "not good" for man to be alone (Genesis 2:18)—this is the only time in the Creation account that God made this statement. In fact, only when God had made both man and woman did he call his work "very good" (Genesis 1:31). In light of these Scriptures and based on his study of the Hebrew term for helpmate, which is *ezer*, a friend of ours offered a good analogy to illustrate the role of the woman as a helpmate. Imagine you are working on a house project, and your 5-year old comes and asks, "Daddy, can I help?" You might respond, "Um, well, sure. Hold that screwdriver for me and hand it to me when I need it, OK?" Do you really *need* the "help"? No. But it is a form of help nonetheless.

Alternatively, suppose that you are hiking with a partner and you lose your footing, slipping down a steep cliff. You grasp onto a rock outcropping and are dangling in mid-air. You cannot pull yourself up in your own strength…you need help! So your partner runs over, gives you his hand, and pulls you up. This second example of "help" is more in line with the definition of "helpmate" than the first. God gave woman to man as an able-bodied assistant—as one who would make him complete; hopefully this simple illustration will help men to honor and respect their wives' roles and contributions within the family unit.

Using the journey analogy, we can simply summarize the biblical teaching this way: mothers are passengers in the car. They are in the front seat alongside of their husbands and they act as co-navigators, but they're not driving. In fact, if they try to control the route by jerking the wheel or stomping on the brake pedal, you can expect an accident. Not only that, but if the second-in-command becomes a "backseat driver," no one enjoys the journey!

This father-led family is certainly the biblical ideal, and God designed it that way for his good purposes. With that said, however, there are circumstances in life that may render a family unable to follow this traditional model. While the role of a single parent (father, mother, or other primary caregiver) will, by default, be that much more difficult than a two-parent model, it's not impossible for you, as a single parent, to successfully emancipate your children *and* receive God's blessings by following his ways.

If you find yourself in such a situation, rest assured that the principles and systems that we share here can still be applied to your family. You will likely have to make additional sacrifices that a two-parent household may not have to. Equally as likely, your task will often seem like an even greater burden. Look for others who can help share your load, and turn to the One who is the source of our strength. He has promised to be a father to the fatherless and to look after the orphan and widow; God has great compassion on all who turn to him for help in their time of need (see, for example, Deuteronomy 10:18, Psalm 10:14, Isaiah 54:4-6).

Let's now look at some of the essentials of family leadership.

God wants drivers. The driver of the vehicle is the ultimate decision-maker. He decides whether the car full of passengers will sit in the driveway or actually get out on the road. He determines where the pit-stops will be, and how long to stay at each pull-off. Whether the car is parked or driving, the person in the driver's seat is still in control. When it comes to family leadership, one of the realities is this: *inaction* is an action and *indecision* is a decision.

What we *don't* do as parents is equally as important as what we *do*. If we as parents, with all good intentions, take our children to church for one hour a week on Sunday without ensuring a healthy environment for the remaining 167 hours, we are certainly not guaranteeing success.

In God's eyes, we are fully responsible for *everything* that our children are taught. This includes not only what *we teach*, but what we allow our children to *be taught*. Silence, or a lack of action, in any area (education, spiritual and ethical training, etc.) leaves voids—and these voids get filled, by default, by society and by people around us. What we *do not do* as parents will shape our children's futures just as much as what we actively *do*.

It becomes important for us, then, to be proactive in decision-making and to remain *in motion* as much as possible. Just as it's difficult to steer a parked car (or for a stalled car to get to its final destination), so the family leader must be committed to *going*. If we're moving, God can steer us—even if we take wrong turns here and there—but if we're parked we'll never get to our destination!

Fathers are in the pole position. The Scriptures tell us that we, as parents, are to be our children's primary *spiritual* teachers, though we may also utilize additional supports like church school or children's Sunday school programs. Our responsibility in spiritual training is non-transferable. The Bible tells us,

> "you must commit yourselves wholeheartedly to these commands I am giving you today. Repeat them again and again to your children. Talk about them when you are at home and when you are away on a journey, when you are lying down and when you are getting up again." (Deuteronomy 6:6-7, NLT)

Since fathers are given responsibility over the family as a whole, this spiritual training becomes their duty. We see this emphasized in Ephesians 6:4: "Fathers, do not exasperate your children; instead, bring them up in the training and instruction of the Lord."

Every voyage begins with a vision. A journey is uniquely imagined and planned in the mind of the traveler before its first steps are taken. Likewise, a family leader should have an inspirational vision in mind for his family. As Christians, our greatest joy is in training up children who will choose to live God's way by their own free will—not out of fear of parental punishment, but rather out of a commitment to serve God faithfully. We want to touch our children's hearts and lead them to a relationship with the Lord that is reflected in their daily living.

The world measures successful emancipation in many ways, including financial autonomy, ethical integrity, and academic skill. We may also emphasize these outcomes in raising our children, but from God's perspective it doesn't matter if our children score a 1600 on their SATs, get a 4.0 at Harvard School of Law or are millionaires at age 23. God's desire, first and foremost, is that our children have a relationship with him and are committed to living in his ways.

Define the destination. Our vision for family success includes the emancipation of our children, and also incorporates the accomplishment of God's purposes—both for the family and for his church.

A 1994 study tabulated the percentages of faithful children (defined by regular, irregular, or non-church attendance) that were emancipated from different households: those with non-practicing fathers and faithful mothers, those with practicing fathers and non-practicing mothers, and those with two faithful parents. One of the more surprising conclusions that arose from this study said:

> "In short, if a father does not go to church, no matter how faithful his wife's devotions, only one child in 50 will become a regular worshipper. If a father does go regularly, regardless of the practice of the mother, between two-thirds and three-quarters of their children will become church-goers (regular and irregular). If a father goes but irregularly to church, regardless of his wife's devotion, between a half and two-thirds of their offspring will find themselves coming to church regularly or occasionally."[1]

Although this study focuses on church attendance as the only measure of both the parents' and the children's faithfulness, this is still a very good indicator of the importance of the father's household leadership, particularly in regard to spiritual matters. The trend of the study clearly shows that fewer and fewer people are committing to the church and to serving God's purposes in the next generation. Fathers, this is our burden to bear—the future of our children hinges upon how we train them in the ways of the Lord. Don't shift that responsibility to others—it is *our* job!

Single parents, however, should not despair in reading these statistics. As a single parent, you accept the responsibility for your children's spiritual training. If you faithfully labor for the Lord, certainly the outcome of your child-rearing is not as cut-and-dry (nor likely as discouraging) as the numbers from this study might indicate. We believe that the study speaks to the necessity of fathers taking a leadership role *within a two-parent household*, and only within that model do its conclusions gain significance.

We're in for the long haul. The family journey is more like a cross-country escapade than a trip down to the local grocery store. The great news is that we have a good 18 to 20 years to get it right—that is, to instill God's precepts into our children's hearts. Occasional parenting blunders (and we all have our moments!) will not derail the process. Long-term consistency in the message and the delivery will ensure our success. Our job is to end well. Low points along the way are expected and need not be a discouragement. They are just opportunities for us to point out to our children that we, too, are

---

[1] Lowe, Fr. Robbie. "How Fatherhood is Crucial to Children's Faith." Reprinted from AD 2000, Vol.16, No. 9 (October 2003), p. 10. *http://www.ad2000.com.au/articles/2003/oct2003p10_1457.html*

not perfect, and regroup. Our job is just to stay the course and take the *LEAD*.

Expect to shift gears. If we as fathers serve the Lord, our own relationship with the Lord is likely to provide spiritual protection for our children. As we walk in faithfulness, they will be more likely to follow our example. We read, "He who fears the LORD has a secure fortress, and for his children it will be a refuge" (Proverbs 14:24).

One challenge that arises in family leadership, however, is that there are two different dynamics at work. In the first phase of parenting, when our children are young, parenting is simply training those under our authority to *do* something—live by particular values, adopt certain routines and behaviors, etc. This is an *authoritative* relationship. This is the type of relationship that God initially had with his chosen people, the Israelites. (We will often refer to this covenant as the *law*.) Here God developed with his children a relationship based on rules, which if adhered to promised blessings (rewards) and if broken promised curses (punishment). See, for example, Exodus 34:10 and Leviticus 26.

However, God did not remain in an authoritative relationship with his children—and neither do we. Some 2,000 years ago God replaced this first covenant with a new covenant—a covenant of grace, which is now available to all humanity (see Jeremiah 31:31-34). This covenant is of the Spirit; it is a heart covenant. It establishes us in a personal relationship with God, wherein we can approach him freely. We are invited into fellowship with God, through Christ.

This is the type of relationship that we emulate with our children as they grow. Our children are slowly given more and more choice and grace. More important than enforcing rules, in this phase, is encouraging them to *want* to live in the ways we have modeled and trained. At this point, our goal is to have them *choose* to do the things that are best and most pleasing to God.

These two biblical examples of covenant relationship become for us a picture of how God wants us to raise our children. Emancipation means transitioning them from *our* authority to *God's* authority—moving them from *rules* to *relationship*. As the ways of the Lord are trained, more and more autonomy is given, as children prepare to leave the "nest" and enter the second covenant phase of their life. This is why adolescence and young-adulthood is so complicated—that's when the transfer from parental authority to personal authority under God takes place. Impressing God's precepts upon their hearts *prior* to this phase is critical.

The Bible says, "Train a child in the way he should go and when he is old he will not depart from it" (Proverbs 22:6). Successful parenting, according to this verse, means preparing our children's hearts to receive God's wisdom so that they choose to live by his precepts when they are on their own. Parents who have emancipated children that serve God faithfully experience tremendous peace and joy in knowing that their perseverance in parenting has paid off; likewise, wayward children result in the exact opposite emotions. This book was written to provide you with biblical wisdom and practical methods that will promote the desired outcome.

REFLECTIONS

Questions:
1. Our family model is likely to be shaped by our own life experiences, particularly by our childhood. How has your view of household leadership been affected by these past experiences? Has God's Word changed your perspective?

Practical Applications and *Additional Resources:*
It can be difficult to make changes in an existing model of family leadership, but with God and with your own personal commitment to change, it is possible! If you have the desire to bring your household more into line with God's Word in this area, check out *The Vision Forum*. The mission of this organization is to rebuild Christian family culture, in part by encouraging parents to embrace their biblical roles within the family. Their website at www.visionforum.com offers a variety of resources for assistance and encouragement, or mail them at 4719 Blanco Road, San Antonio, TX 78212.

For Further Study:
During your Bible study time, ask God to speak to you through some of the biblical examples of family leadership (or lack thereof) that are given in his Word. Just a few suggestions: Noah (Genesis 7), Eli (1 Samuel 3 and 4), and Nabal (1 Samuel 25). How might these truths change you?

Chapter 3: The Compass that Guides us

Even if the Bible is our roadmap—and a perfect one, at that—we can still experience frustration in getting to its pinpointed destination. One problem may be that we just don't read maps well (perhaps it's upside-down and we don't even realize it). Maybe we get disoriented with directions and don't see how this thing on paper applies to our actual driving route. Or, maybe it's a world map when we'd benefit more from a local street map. Just as these obstacles with map-reading can keep us from successfully navigating our way from point A to point B, we see that having the Bible as our guide in life's travels does not, in itself, guarantee a successful journey. In the end, it's not a problem with *the map* that causes difficulty; it may be that its level of detail seems overwhelming to our need, we simply have difficulty understanding it, or perhaps we are unable to practically apply its information to our circumstances.

For us, at one time or another, all of these challenges applied. We believed in the authority of Scripture and were committed to living as God desired for us. Yet, the Bible is a big book with a lot of information, making it difficult for the average person to apply in specific circumstances without a lot of time and effort committed to study. Likewise, sometimes we knew what the Bible said, but weren't sure what was best to do with the information.

As we devoted more and more time to the study of the Word, however, particularly as it applied to successful family living, we saw some revealing trends emerge. As we read, we found hundreds of Scriptures and examples of people of faith who were promised—and given—success, peace, joy, and other abundant blessings as they lived according to God's Word. Putting case studies and specific verses together, we saw that all of the individuals who were most used, and most blessed, by God were those who lived their lives according to 12 fundamental values—we coined these "the 12 core values of God," or, *the values that God values.* People who live out these values exhibit a godly character that the Lord rewards.

For us, identifying these foundational character traits was akin to digesting all of the information in a complex road map such that we could rely on a compass for quick directions and assurance that we're on the right track in our travels. The 12 core values have become that compass. They point us in the direction of successful emancipation for our children *and* God's blessings for ourselves as we strive to live according to his Word. We still need to know what his Word says, to be sure, but the core values provide just the right sort of pointed and sure guidance we need, on a moment-by-moment basis, so that we can remain on-course in the more specific route that's already mapped.

As family leaders, we are called to *live out* these godly values for ourselves. The apostle Paul instructed his young protégé, Timothy, "...train yourself to be godly. For... godliness has value for all things, holding promise for both the present life and the life to come..." (1 Timothy 4:7b-8). As we grow in godliness, we become more effective in serving God and his purposes.

Further, our goal as parents should be to *train* our children in these key character traits that are important to God. Doing so will ensure that our children have the proper foundations for living according to God's precepts prior to emancipation. In fact, we see that Paul *also* told Timothy to "command and teach these things" (1 Timothy 4:11). As we live out the values that reflect a godly character, we are to train our children in these truths as well.

It is important, then, to be proactive in both living out and training our children in the values that God values. In doing so, we will shape them according to the timeless principles of God's Word and encourage them in Christlikeness. They will be equipped to fulfill God's purposes as they mature.

As you undergo the unending process of character training with your children, remember that the goal is to transition them from *rules* to *relationship*. Living according to God's Word may begin as a law, but in the end it must be the desire of our children's hearts. Balanced training helps to accomplish this objective. Suggested methods for impressing godly values on our children's hearts will be discussed in much more detail in Part Two of this book.

The next logical question is, *what are the values that God values?* Certainly, the answer to this question is of utmost importance, for it affects nearly everything we do as parents within a values-driven paradigm. Seeking out God's values is vital, because if we approach values training from a worldly perspective or with our own human wisdom, we may be missing the mark. In spite of our best efforts, we may still fail to fulfill God's purposes for this and the next generation.

Romans 8:29 reveals that Christlikeness is God's ultimate objective for his people: "For those God foreknew he also predestined to be conformed to the likeness of his Son..." God desires that we *do what Jesus did*, and, more importantly, that we *exhibit his character*.

In its simplest form, *doing what Jesus did* means living out the expressed purposes of the church. Exhibiting the character of Christ, however, is slightly more complicated.

In the Bible, Jesus is referred to as the Word in the flesh: "In the beginning was the Word, and the Word was with God, and the Word was God...The Word became flesh and made his dwelling among us" (John 1:1 and 14). We see that *all* of the teachings of the Scriptures were made manifest in the person of Jesus Christ. Therefore, a study of his character will lead us to explore the whole of God's Word, not just the small segment of Scripture that describes his life on earth.

In studying the whole of Scripture as an expression of the fullness of Christ, we see that the 12 core values do, indeed, define his character. The evidence for these core values comes not just from the gospel accounts of Jesus' life, but also from the overall teachings of Scripture and from character studies of key men and women who walked closely with God. These 12 biblical core values are: *faith, surrender, love, faithfulness, wisdom, self-control, righteousness, humility, holiness, diligence, generosity* and *praise.*

Ultimately, these core values represent essential character traits that God wants to manifest in his people. These are the values that God values. Living them out helps us grow in Christlikeness and equips us to fulfill God's purposes. As we do so, God shows us his favor, for as Proverbs 10:6 (NLT) tells us, "the godly are showered with blessings."

Certainly, even without the Lord, people *can* operate in many of the core values and see the benefits thereof; however, this success is without lasting significance unless it is given by God (see Ecclesiastes 1:1-2, Ecclesiastes 2:24-26, Ecclesiastes 12). Those who work diligently can earn rewards from their labor; people who walk in wisdom can achieve great success; those who persevere in righteousness (even self-defined righteousness) can find reward for their good character. If even an unbeliever practices self-control, she will avoid the many pitfalls associated with destructive behaviors: addiction, sexual sin, poor health, etc.

Likewise, core values such as love that operate according to the law of reciprocity can also bring benefits to the believers and non-believers alike who live accordingly. For example, even the unfaithful receive love from those to whom they show love.

Because many of the core values *can* be lived apart from God—and bring temporal rewards—a lot of personal success gurus have become extremely popular. You may find a great deal of truth in their materials. Their methods work, however, because *God* made them to work! Remember, the prosperity of the unfaithful is only temporary (see Proverbs 13:22). Without faith and surrender, worldly gain is fleeting. Those who achieve personal success may enjoy this life, but they have no promise for the next. Because they lack a right relationship with God, many of these prosperous individuals will still feel empty and unsettled. The worldly benefits they experience by living a "good" life are but poor reflections of God-given blessings: happiness rather than joy, worldly security rather than inner peace, material success rather than godly prosperity (which may simply amount to being content in all circumstances or always having what we need).

The real deal only comes from operating in all of God's core values. We are certain to miss the fullness of the abundant life God has for us if we pick and choose which values feel right for us, or if we live by the good teachings without putting our trust in God himself.

In this values-driven paradigm, we are partners with God. God's will is accomplished in and through us, as both we and our children live in ways that please him. As we cooperate with God, we will receive the rich rewards of success, peace, and joy that his Word promises—both in this life and in the age to come. What a great opportunity we have! If we will simply choose to persevere in abiding by his precepts, we will be richly blessed. God is faithful and will stand by his promises for us; we just need to do our part.

In Part Three of this book we'll be exploring the 12 core values in depth, to practically apply the biblical teachings of these characteristics to everyday family life.

REFLECTIONS

Questions:
1. Think about some of the values that you were modeled and taught throughout your childhood: both *positive* values and *negative* ones. Was there consistency between your parents' values training and their lifestyle?
2. What values are you unconsciously modeling for your children, and are these at odds with what you are trying to teach?

Practical Applications and *Additional Resources:*

If you want to grow in Christlikeness and get to the next level in your spiritual walk, get yourself a copy of *The Values-Driven Life: Accelerated Growth for the Christian Soul*. In it you will be taken, in detail, through each of the 12 core values presented in this book. The book makes an excellent personal or family devotional. To learn more about it, read reviews, or order a copy, visit www.valuesdrivenlife.com.

For Further Study:

The Bible identifies many men and women who lived out God's values and experienced great success as they remained faithful to the Lord and his Word. Just a few examples are Joseph (Genesis 39), Daniel (Daniel 6), and Joshua (Joshua 1). Study these examples, or find some others on your own, and see how these individuals lived the core values and reflected godly character.

Part One: The Journey to Family Success

Chapter 4: Are We There Yet?

Before we commit to going on a long trip, we are usually careful to check out the vehicle we will be driving. We make sure it's been tuned up, the brakes are good, the oil has been changed, and so on. Certainly, if there are mechanical problems, we would hesitate to take the car on the road, particularly for an extended drive.

Likewise, before we embark on our family journey, we must consider our vehicle. Is it solid and dependable? Will it get us where we are going—safely, and with minimal difficulty? For us, the vehicle we depend on in our journey is *discipline*—it's what carries us from point A to point B. We don't mean the discipline that results from misbehavior, but rather, a proactive *self-discipline*. This is synonymous with dedication and resolution. Self-discipline is the committed effort that sustains us in the 18-year goal of successfully emancipating our children, and in achieving God's purposes for our family in the midst of daily challenges.

The Bible confirms the need for this focused determination in the apostle Paul's reference to a race. He writes, "Do you not know that in a race all the runners run, but only one gets the prize? Run in such a way as to get the prize." And he tells us how this is accomplished: "Everyone who competes in the games goes into strict training....Therefore I do not run like a man running aimlessly; I do not fight like a man beating the air" (see 1 Corinthians 9:24-27). God wants us to give his call our best effort.

As we strive to reach our goals as parents, however, we should remember that God is not after perfection—he simply wants our willingness to pursue his ways. *Seeking God's direction is perfection!* If we have a heart that wants to do it God's way, he will honor that. If we commit *our* best, God will deliver *his* best. This is illustrated by God's promised rewards for those who willingly embrace his covenant:

> "When you, *on your part*, will obey these directives, keeping and following them, GOD, *on his part*, will keep the covenant of loyal love that he made with your ancestors: He will love you, he will bless you, he will increase you. He will bless the babies from your womb and the harvest of grain, new wine, and oil from your fields; he'll bless the calves from your herds and lambs from your flocks in the country he promised your ancestors that he'd give you" (Deuteronomy 7:12-13, MSG, italics added for emphasis).

I (Cindy) often get up early to spend quiet time with the Lord before beginning my day. I have found it to be a necessary self-discipline, and I value the investment I'm making in my relationship with God. This set-apart time prepares me for the busyness of each day.

If my sleep has been disrupted throughout the night, however (and what mother's isn't, on occasion?), I may find myself feeling exhausted during the day. Keeping up with housework, home school, and little ones is more likely to be irritating and frustrating. Usually, as well, these are the days when the children seem to be testing all the known limits! At these times, I have to remind myself of the importance of self-discipline: of keeping my feelings in check, of keeping a tight reign on my tongue, and even of taking a nap in the afternoon if I need it. My mood affects the atmosphere of the entire household, and when I am at my weakest, emotionally or physically, those are the times when the necessity of *discipline* becomes obvious if I'm going to persevere in being the person God wants me to be and in fulfilling his purposes for my life.

Likewise, we all have moments along the journey in which we're tempted to give up, or when obstacles spring up in our path and we may stumble and fall. These times are inevitable—but God uses them to help us grow in Christlikeness. They may also be opportunities for us to affirm our godly character, or as the apostle Paul put it, to "live up to what we have already attained" (Philippians 3:16). This demands a great deal of perseverance in less-than-perfect life's circumstances. We can be assured, however, that as we progress, God takes note of our efforts: "I know all the things you do--your love, your faith, your service, and your patient endurance. And I can see your constant improvement in all these things" (Revelation 2:19, NLT).

Let's briefly return to Paul's "race" metaphor and see how it can encourage us in our family journey.

Family life is not a sprint; it's a marathon. Paul tells the Philippian church that he has committed himself to "focusing all my energies on this one thing: Forgetting the past and looking forward to what lies ahead, I strain to reach the end of the race and receive the prize for which God, through Christ Jesus, is calling us up to heaven" (Philippians 3:13-14, NLT).

Paul was a "sprinter." In reading the gospel accounts of the life of Jesus, we can see that Jesus was a sprinter, too. Both were single men committed to God's service, and they did not have the hindrance of divided interests (namely, family responsibilities) preventing them from fully serving God (see 1 Corinthians 7:32). They had grandiose missions with a short timetable. They are perfect examples of living the life of faith, fully committed to God.

But what about those of us who serve God, yet recognize that we *do* have divided interests? What about caring for our wives and training our children? We are not, by default, disqualified for the prize, simply because we cannot press toward the mark at the same break-neck pace. Let's face it, we just aren't running the same race. We are not sprinters at all—we are running a marathon!

The married man's race: balancing the family and God's service. A marathon is considerably different from a sprint. Generally, a sprint is an all-out run for the entire duration of the race. It doesn't require as much technical strategy to perform. Marathon runners *do* sprint during some of the race; however, they have to pace themselves in order to finish well. This is a good description of the Christian family leader, and is much different from the type of race we see both Paul and Jesus running as they pursued God's call on their lives. We *can* live out God's purposes—but we're also training our children to do the same. For this reason, the pace will likely (by default) be a little bit slower. This should not be a cause for concern. Don't forget, part of our race is the "relay" aspect of passing along our faith to our children.

It takes discipline to finish well. Because we are running a marathon in serving God and in training our children to do likewise, our committed effort is vital for victory. Hebrews 12:1 reveals the importance of self-discipline in staying the course: "… let us throw off everything that hinders and the sin that so easily entangles, and let us run with perseverance the race marked out for us."

Finishing well is the goal, and it does take some discipline to get to our desired end. But it is all worth it! Although sending children out into the world faithfully serving God is its own reward, there are additional blessings that we can depend on as we run the race. In fact, the beauty of the family "marathon" is that it's not all just sweat and effort. We will experience runner's high during much of the run if we cooperate with God. There *are* inclines and headwinds, but there are also downhill stretches, the wind on our backs and that refreshing "second wind."

Resolve to follow God's way and he will see to it that you succeed. Philippians 1:6 tells us, "…he who began a good work in you will carry it on to completion." This promise, and others like it, should give us much confidence as we run the race during those difficult periods.

Stay on course—God's way is the best way. The track we are running may seem endless, or obstacles may spring up in our path. We *will* be tempted to give up. Paul puts it this way: "You were running superbly! Who cut in on you, deflecting you from the true course of obedience? This detour doesn't come from the One who called you into the race in the first place" (Galatians 5:7-8, MSG). God's way is the best way—but that doesn't mean it's always easy. Yet God is faithful and will give us his strength in our times of weakness. The Lord assured Paul, "'My grace is sufficient for you, for my power is made perfect in weakness.'" As a result, Paul was content with his shortcomings and trusted God through his trials: "for Christ's sake, I delight in weaknesses, in insults, in hardships, in persecutions, in difficulties. For when I am weak, then I am strong" (2 Corinthians 12:9-10).

The Values-Driven Family

Encouragement for the journey. Discipline helps us live a happier, healthier, more purposeful family life. Certainly, it takes effort to make progress in areas where we see deficiencies. But anything worth having is worth working for, and God will give us the grace to persevere, no matter what our past experience has been. *The Message* paraphrase puts it this way: "if you embrace the way God does things, there are wonderful payoffs... without regard to where you are from or how you were brought up" (Romans 2:10).

If you want better things for your children (and what parent doesn't?), just *make a commitment* to *making progress*—in one area at a time, and one small step at a time. The practical examples and suggestions that we will offer throughout the remainder of this book are designed to help you do just that.

So stay the course, and remember—it's not just about *accomplishment*, it's about *progress*. Remember that the values-driven family is an 18-year plan. Focus on the long-range vision rather than the daily grind, and you'll see that there's plenty of time to reach your goals, even with those bumps in the road. Even if you take two steps forward and one step back, you'll still be moving ahead. So don't think in terms of what you didn't get done, or how far you have left to go; think in terms of how much progress you have made. Paul reminded Timothy that committed effort would advance his journey of faith: "be diligent in these matters; give yourself wholly to them, so that everyone may see your progress" (1 Timothy 4:15). Likewise, our consistent self-discipline will draw us ever nearer to our final destination.

REFLECTIONS

Questions:
1. What are some of the things that tempt you to "give up" as you run your family race?
2. Think about some defining moments when you have been the most discouraged—what prompted you to keep going?

For Further Study:
Most of the biblical references to discipline refer to the Lord's discipline of us as his children, the goal of which is to make us more like Christ (see Hebrews 12:10, for example). Proverbs 1:1-3, 2 Timothy 1:7, and Titus 1:8, however, use the word *discipline* to refer to the self-discipline that we've defined as an essential part of the family journey. Using a concordance or other reference tools, explore the definitions and implications of the various uses of the word *discipline*.

Chapter 5: "Mom, I'm Hungry!"

We know where we're going and the car seems ready to go. We don't want to be running late in getting to our destination, so we rush everyone into the car, buckle all those seatbelts and secure all the car seats—and off we go! Yet we're not on the road very long before someone says, "I have to go to the bathroom!" You realize that you forgot to go through the last-minute "everyone use the bathroom before we leave" routine. Following that train of thought, it hits you that *you forgot the diaper bag*! And it's almost lunch time, but there aren't even any snacks in the car.

Just as in our travels we are wise to consider things such as food, fuel, and time considerations, so too, in our family journey, should we think about our provisions and their proper apportionment. This element of the family journey is the *stewardship* that guides us in our travels. We only have a certain number of hours in each day, and only so much strength and energy. Likewise, there's only so much money. Yes, these resources will deplete and be re-stocked, but we need to be sure we're using them wisely and properly addressing our family's priorities.

In our early Christian walk, we mostly associated the term *stewardship* with financial accountability. Later, we were introduced to the concept of stewarding our talents and time as well. All of these aspects of stewardship became important to us along our own family journey.

In putting together all of these different elements, and in seeing how to apply the various teachings on biblical stewardship in the context of family, we've come to broadly define the term *stewardship* as *balance:* balancing our time and our money, balancing the practical aspects of family with God's purposes, and so on.

Certainly, we want to be good stewards because it helps us to maximize our effectiveness, but ultimately it is our heart's desire because God calls us to be good stewards with the resources he has entrusted to us. This is clear in Jesus' parable of the talents (see Matthew 25:14-30). In this biblical illustration, the two servants who multiplied their resources were commended, while the one who had buried his talent (earning no return) was severely chastised by his master.

Good, better, best: balancing our decisions.

Life is nothing but a series of decisions; as good stewards of what God gives us, we will seek a godly balance in making all of the decisions pertinent to family life. Achieving this balance means considering what is *good, better,* and *best* in every situation. There are always multiple ways of addressing different issues, but a good steward will be committed to choosing God's best. And God promises that he will help us in this: "I am the LORD your God, who teaches you what is best for you, who directs you in the way you should go" (Isaiah 48:17-18).

The whole of Scripture teaches a lot that can help us to choose God's best in many areas of life. There are countless verses that, together, cover just about every aspect of family life.

God's Word is true and dependable, and will never contradict itself. However, as we seek God's best through the guidance of Scripture, it may seem difficult to know what God is saying. We find that using the Scriptures to help us make daily decisions means that the art of *balance* must further come into play. We should consider how specific *verses* of Scripture fit into its *overall teachings*. A balanced view of the Scriptures means that we will not always be able to define "right" or "wrong." Instead, we are more likely to see situations in terms of *good, better,* and *best*.

The Bible says, "everything is permissible, but not everything is beneficial" (1 Corinthians 6:12). This is a key verse in understanding how the concept of *good, better, best* applies; it reveals that, ultimately, there are shades of gray when it comes to everyday biblical living. Please don't misunderstand—this *does not* mean that anyone is permitted to sin. The Bible is rather clear on what is sinful and what is righteous. However, it *does* mean that there is considerable flexibility in how we are to live life in issues not pertaining to salvation and righteousness.

Examples of choice in the area of family life include: mom work full time, part time, or remain at home; public school, private school, or home school; unrestricted TV, restricted TV, or no TV. The issues are many, but certainly you see the point. These are not necessarily matters of right and wrong. There are Scripture verses that can give us guidance and help us make our decisions, yet the Holy Spirit and our conscience will ultimately be what convicts us as to what is most appropriate (or, *best*) for us. In Part Four of this book, we'll explore some specific family situations in light of this *good, better, best* stewardship paradigm.

Balance in Our Actions

The stewardship of *balance* is a key to success in decision-making *and* in living out those decisions. Ecclesiastes 7:18 tells us, "The man who fears God will avoid all extremes."

As family leaders, we oversee all aspects of life, including *work*, *family*, *ministry*, and *rest*. All of our time, treasure and talents are to be applied to these four areas; they form what we call the four "quadrants" of family life. In order to achieve God's purposes for this generation and the next, no one area can be overemphasized, nor can any area be neglected; *balance* in our actions becomes more important than ever.

If we over-emphasize work, we can certainly be good stewards with our treasure; yet, we run the risk of sacrificing family relationships, ministry, and even personal rest. If ministry is our focus, we may fail to minister to our own families and to the heart needs of our children. Again, other aspects of life can be put in jeopardy.

There also are risks associated with too great a focus on rest, or leisure. We can spend too much time watching TV, and not enough time building our family relationships or serving God. Certainly, one who is heavily invested in leisure can also experience problems with working diligently, as God desires.

Likewise, it's a fallacy to think that an over-emphasis on family is all good—balance is needed in this area, too. In a child-centric home, parents may frantically chaperone their children from one activity to the next, believing that they are doing the "best" for their children, but they may not commit enough time, talent, or treasure to achieving God's purposes now. The children are given the best the world has to offer, but they may not receive all that God has to offer.

These examples may represent some extremes. However, you will likely see some elements of one of these scenarios in your own family. The point to be emphasized is that each of the four quadrants of life needs its due attention in order for us to live balanced lives and be effective in achieving God's objectives. We are called to be wise stewards of the resources God has entrusted to us: time, money, and ability. As such, we should seek the proper balance in decision-making and in implementing those decisions.

REFLECTIONS

Questions:
1. What are some of the possible obstacles that might keep you from living a more balanced, biblical family life? Consider your own attitudes (such as skepticism, pride, laziness, indifference, etc.) as well as social expectations and norms and your current circumstances.

Practical Applications and *Additional Resources:*
Visit our blog (http://valuesdrivenfamily.blogspot.com) for practical helps in achieving a better-balanced family life. We also offer many FREE resources at our website, www.valuesdrivenfamily.com.

For Additional Study:

If you've had difficulty in making the Bible relevant to a particular life situation, go back and re-visit that situation. Engage in some in-depth study, using Bible study references if necessary. Ask God to give you a balanced view of his Word and, possibly, a new perspective on how to read or apply his truth. If applicable, explore the situation and Scriptures in light of the *good, better, best* paradigm.

Part One: The Journey to Family Success

Chapter 6: The Journey Begins

Now we've looked at all the foundations for family success: *leadership, values, discipline,* and *stewardship.* These four enduring elements will affect our family journey, both how we live out God's core values for ourselves and how we teach those values to our children. With these things thoughtfully considered, however, it becomes an easier task to live out this values-driven life.

It seems obvious that if you have read this far, you truly want God's best for your family. However, reading this book is just a first step. Doing what God desires is the more important part of the journey.

Please take a moment to get a proper perspective on yourself and your family situation. Think about what may be keeping you from embracing a biblical family paradigm and pursuing God's purposes for yourself and your family. Be honest with yourself and with God, and be open to what God wants to speak to you through his Word and through this book.

No matter what you read, realize that there is no quick fix. Change comes gradually through the power of the Holy Spirit at work within you. Be encouraged that God does not expect you to do it all at once. As you read, continually seek him to see what he would have you work on in yourself or in your family. You may need to take drastic steps, or you may choose smaller steps. But be committed, and don't give up! Strive to make progress, and remember that *seeking God's direction is perfection!*

It is our prayer that the remainder of this book will help you along on your journey to becoming a more values-driven family. We hope that God will show you an abundance of peace, joy and success as you apply his precepts to your life and seek his best.

We have found that God has shown us much grace in our journey. Although we have not yet reached our destination, he continues to guide us day by day. As we've continued to do our best to live out the concepts presented in this book, we feel as though God has showered us with blessings—in greater measure than we would ever have thought possible.

With the promise of all that—and more—as you strive to align your family life with God's good Word, let's continue our journey together.

The next part of this book will focus on your biblical responsibilities as parents: *training, encouragement,* and *discipline.* Addressing all three of these aspects of parenting, in balance, will be the impetus for the successful emancipation of your children. We address this subject first because it is usually the destination that every parent wants to arrive at on this family journey.

Part Three will give you a biblical perspective on the 12 core values of God, and you'll see the many blessings that God has in store for you as you commit to living according to these precepts from his Word. Because the *training* element of our biblical parenting model rests upon these specific values, we'll also include some teachable verses and practical applications to help you not only model the values for your children but actively teach them as well. This values-driven living is what will help you and your whole family to not only arrive at your destination but also to *enjoy the journey*.

Part Four will offer some practical applications, from a project management perspective, that address many of the concerns of everyday family living. We've leveraged some time-tested principles that have been widely accepted in the business world to aid us in managing our household. We'll share some of the different systems and strategies that we've implemented that have helped us to become more effective and achieve greater joy, peace, and success in daily life. This is where the rubber hits the road in regard to living out God's values and purposes in the context of family.

Jesus modeled leadership and loving service for his disciples by washing their feet. After he had done this, he said to them, "You know these things-- now do them! That is the path of blessing" (John 13:17, NLT). Likewise, you'll see the most success, peace, and joy along your family journey as you commit to living out God's values and purposes for your life.

PART TWO: The Parenting Part of the Journey

"Tell [them all] these things. Urge (advise, encourage, warn) and rebuke with full authority. Let no one despise or disregard or think little of you [conduct yourself and your teaching so as to command respect]." (Titus 2:15, AMP)

Bringing our children to emancipation with a sincere heart to obey and follow the Lord is our ultimate goal as faithful parents. Personally, we've read many expert theories on how this is best accomplished, but had become increasingly frustrated by the seeming incompleteness of each resource. Some focused on biblical training but we didn't find enough of the practical that would help us address the everyday "non-spiritual" issues. Other methods offered some good application, such as with behavioral charts and reward systems, but neglected to provide a solid scriptural foundation for their implementation. Likewise, some taught that discipline was all-important, and with that in place, everything else would just sort of happen by default. Trying to piece it all together was impossible.

So, as we went along on this parenting adventure, we tried different things at different times, and we also studied the Bible to find out more about what God said. Slowly but surely, he showed us how all the pieces fit. Much like the "journey" analogy expressed our desires for biblical family living, God also gave us a little word-picture for parenting.

Successful, biblical parenting is like a 3-legged stool. The stool will not bear weight, or remain stable, unless all three legs are present and solid. Those three legs are *training, encouragement,* and *discipline.* It takes all three to succeed—and in that order. In this section, we'll share with you the biblical foundations for these three elements and offer some personal examples to share our experience. We'll also provide you with some practical suggestions and systems to help you balance it all and experience the maximum of joy, peace, and success in this parenting journey.

Chapter 7: Pointing Our Kids in the Right Direction: *Training*

Quite likely, most Christian parents have heard time and again the biblical admonition to "train up a child in the way he should go: and when he is old, he will not depart from it" (Proverbs 22:6, KJV). *The Message* paraphrase puts a refreshing twist on this often-repeated proverb—and we even see its application to the metaphor of our family journey: "point your kids in the right direction—when they're old they won't be lost." Biblical training is what will keep our children faithfully following God's path throughout their life's journey.

We've likened the 12 core values of God to a compass that keeps us headed in the right direction, even if we're not in a place where we can study our map. As such, these values have become a valuable tool in our child-training regimen and have allowed us to instill God's values and precepts on our children's hearts in a more consistent manner than Bible teaching alone. The essence of training, after all, is to impress God's commandments upon our children and to "talk about them when [we] sit at home and when [we] walk along the road, when [we] lie down and when [we] get up" (Deuteronomy 6:6-7).

Continuous instruction in God's Word is arguably the most important element of successfully raising children. We are to faithfully share God's Word not only verbally but also through our own consistent modeling; Ephesians 5:1 (AMP) puts it this way: "Therefore be imitators of God [copy Him and follow His example], as well-beloved children [imitate their father]." You've probably heard the expression, *more is caught than taught*—it's true! We're sure we're not the only parents who have seen some of our own character traits magnified in our children—and unfortunately, we cringe at those moments because it's usually not the positive ones that are most evident.

While we aren't expected to be perfect, we should *seek* perfection in order to keep the hearts of our children. As our children see us strive to live by God's ideal, they will follow our example. If, however, they discover a "do as I say, not as I do" mentality, they will be more likely to cast aside the whole of our teaching and training. Sometimes we find it helpful to be transparent with our children about obvious struggles we are facing. From our example, they will learn how to cooperate with the Holy Spirit to change undesirable behaviors. They also learn that we are growing together as a family and we can help each other along through encouragement and prayer. We are constantly reminding ourselves that our modeling of God's Word and his core values is foundational to our successful training of them.

Conditioning as a Foundation for Child Training

From our readings on child training and from our own experience, we've seen two distinct types of *training,* both of which we've tried to capitalize on for maximum effectiveness. In practical application, *training* begins not with direct instruction, but with *conditioning*. The goal of conditioning is to conform our children to certain standards of behavior, before they have the capability of formal reasoning or understanding.

Children are mischievous by nature and will exhibit whatever behaviors are permitted. The longer we wait to engage in training, the more freedom the child believes she has, and the more difficult it becomes for a parent to establish him or herself as an authority. Our first experience with this came when our son, Isaiah, was just nine months old. We had sat him down for dinner in his high chair, which on that night consisted of cut green beans. He'd happily eaten beans on many prior occasions, but for some reason, this time he fussed before even attempting to take a bite; soon, he had overturned his bowl and began to howl.

We persisted in re-presenting the beans, to no avail. We even tried to manually put one in his mouth to give him a "taste" for it, but his lips remained stubbornly clenched shut. Needless to say, we were becoming frustrated, but we also were keenly aware that for us to give in would set a very bad precedent. Nine months old or two years—the age made no difference. He knew what he was doing and he was waiting for us to make a move. In our minds, this first battle would set the stage for whether the war was won or lost for us as parents. We were determined to win.

It was a long and somewhat painful encounter. We let him sit in his high chair and protest the beans for about 45 minutes. Realizing that he wasn't going to just give up, we re-heated the beans and put a little margarine on them. Still no luck.

Finally, we put some of the beans in a totally different bowl, sprinkled them with a little sugar, and forced one into his mouth. That got his attention. As he happily ate those, we re-introduced the first bowl (of plain beans) and he ate them without complaint. We showered him with praise when he had finished them all. To be sure, we had rigged the outcome, but in the end we accomplished our goal and established our authority—that was the important thing.

Early conditioning sets the stage for later instruction and can be either *positive* or *negative* in nature. Examples of negative training include: saying a firm, "No!" to a certain infant behavior, offering a gentle tap on the fingers with a handy implement, or (our personal favorite) a little "flick" with the forefinger and thumb to the hand. This type of conditioning is not appropriate for babies, but rather should begin when a child is able to understand, and comply with, simple instructions. We've found this to be around 10 to 12 months of age—roughly about the time a child is able to walk. To provide positive conditioning, a parent may model appropriate behaviors or repeat desired actions and encourage a child's mimicry of them. It is never too early to start this type of conditioning—in fact, the earlier the better!

We've seen the rewards of positive conditioning as we've gotten in the habit of having daily "training sessions" with our children. These can be as short as five minutes or as long as 20 minutes. During training time, we practice the desired response for certain commands that are associated with commonplace events and activities such as, *line up, get coats and shoes, brush your teeth,* and *sit quietly.* We've also used this method to condition behaviors that may need only occasional addressing, such as older siblings learning gentleness with a new baby or the children putting coats and shoes away in their proper places.

We have fun training in things like cleaning up—the children get to dump a big bin of toys and then "race" to put them away as fast as possible. We've also done some amusing role play to train the children how to politely interrupt when two adults are engaged in conversation. In this scenario, Mom played the role of one adult and we pretended that the crying baby was another adult—the children had to stand politely by and wait for a break in the "crying" before saying, "Excuse me, Mom," and proceeding with their request. They thought it was hilarious! So you can see that training *does* focus on conforming behaviors, but also should be engaging, and even enjoyable, for the children when possible.

The benefit of these anticipatory training sessions is that the children are being conditioned to obey our commands, though they may lack an immediate purpose. We conduct this type of training at a quiet time when we can all focus on expectations and proper behaviors—*before* circumstances force us to deal with disobedience, dawdling, or misunderstanding at a time when it is inconvenient or we feel pressured. This helps to maintain a positive tone in training, and we find that our instruction is very well received in this environment.

Compare this proactive training with the "drill and practice" methodology used by any sporting coach. Players commit to consistent practice, wherein they engage in physical fitness and endurance activities. They also learn and rehearse various game plays to ensure their understanding and mastery of the necessary knowledge and skills. Drill and practice is what prepares athletes for "the big game"; the coach doesn't wait until his team is on the field to tell them what he expects them to do during play.

Another "conditioning" element of training that has been very beneficial for us is the establishment of routines and order by way of scheduling (for feedings, naps, and social times versus independent play). This structure is valuable even for infants, and it also provides boundaries and security for children as they age.

We've seen that this beginning conditioning, in its various forms, is of utmost importance in the overall success of child training because it positions the adult as an authority, rather than allowing the child's whims to rule every circumstance. As a result, the child comes to learn that we are in control and yet have his best interest in mind. Ultimately, a child who respects his parents is more likely to embrace the values that they value and adopt them as his own during the more formal, instructional phase of training.

Teaching as Advanced Training

As children develop intellectually, the element of *teaching* should supplement mere conditioning; this should begin even in a child's infancy. At these early stages, we've used simple stories and rhymes to encourage a basic biblical awareness. We also sing Sunday school or Scripture memory songs. Although neither one of us is musically inclined, I (Cindy) have seen the element of music used effectively in classrooms to reinforce various educational concepts. Try to get that fast food jingle out of your head, and you'll realize that music can keep you thinking about something that you might otherwise forget! As a result, we've acquired a decent selection of favorite Bible songs for our little ones.

Teaching, in this and every developmental phase, also means just *talking* to our children as we go about our day, saying simple things like, "God loves us and he wants us to love each other," "God made the whole world," or "God gave us a beautiful day today. Let's thank him!" The content of our dialogue is obviously adjusted to the intellectual capacity of the child. But we do strive to mimic the Proverbs 31 woman, who is described as "speak[ing] with wisdom" and having "faithful instruction...on her tongue" (Proverbs 31:26).

The Bible as a Foundation for Training

We have made it a point to make time for Bible reading, since this is the foundation of spiritual training. A daily time has been most beneficial for us and we would highly recommend it; however, this does not have to be a lengthy time, nor do you need to make a formal "lesson" out of it. God's Word is alive and active, remember, so all you have to do is read it. You may choose to read a particular book, or you may read topical verses—whatever seems appropriate to you. This should be a fun time.

Here are some tips from our "trenches" on maximizing Bible time with your family:

Keep it simple. Children's attention spans are short, and forcing them to attend to an entire chapter, for example, will only frustrate them and create negative associations with Bible reading altogether.

Just read the Word. Ask a couple of review questions when you are finished, if you would like, or summarize the reading for your children to make sure they got something out of it.

Read with interest. Change the volume, tone, or pitch of your voice to accommodate different speakers or "sounds" (earthquakes or storms are also fun to enact).

Be creative. Try using role play to dramatize Bible stories as you read, with each family member playing a different part. Or, have the children make stick puppets and put on a Bible story puppet show for Mom and Dad.

Choose a Bible translation. If you have a preference, use it. If it is a difficult translation, you may want to slightly paraphrase to make sure that the children understand what is being said. The Living Bible or the New Living Translation, in particular, have been written in a more conversational and understandable form, which may be easier for children to follow.

Make it relevant. Particularly when Bible reading is a new routine for your children, choose passages that are interesting and relevant to their lives. It's also important to use Scripture to help children understand *their* roles within the family: to *honor* their parents (Ephesians 6:2-3), to *obey* parental instructions (Proverbs 6:20, Ephesians 6:1, Colossians 3:20), and to *learn* from their parents' teachings (Proverbs 4:1, Proverbs 13:18, Proverbs 16:20).

We have also encouraged our children to have their own "quiet time" with God's Word, on a daily or regular basis. This may only be 10 or 15 minutes, or it may be longer. Our pre-readers convene together and listen to "The Word & Song Bible," which is very engaging but, we feel, also true to the Scriptures. Alternatively, you could have your children listen to an audiotape or CD reading of the Bible text or simply "read" to themselves from a picture Bible or your own adult Bible.

Older children can read their own Bible or even use a more formal "Bible study." To make sure they are optimizing this time, you can have them write a sentence or two in a journal each day about what was meaningful to them in their reading. Or, they can write down verses to memorize, etc. Alternatively, you could just make it a point to casually discuss their Bible time with them after they have finished.

No matter what your children "do" with Bible time, the idea is for them to develop a reverence and respect for God's Word and understand its importance and authority in their lives. As faithful parents, we want to encourage our children's faithfulness to God by training them in the value of God's Word and the discipline of reading and studying it.

Core Value Training as a Supplement to Bible Teaching

Although the Bible is the foundation for our children's spiritual training, it's an intimidating volume. As such, incorporating it into daily living so that it became impressed upon our children's hearts was a challenge for us—as, we are sure, it is for many parents. As a result, our biblical training regimen has come to rely upon what we call the "core value method." We strive to teach our children each of the values that God values—the 12 that are described in this book. We believe that in so doing they will have on their hearts everything they need to leave our care fully committed to God and his Word.

The whole premise of training by God's core values was born from the knowledge of two facts: first, children have short attention spans and second, the Bible is big. We have used the 12 core values of God as the basis for effective child training because they are pointed references to character traits that are of value to God, *and* they have Scripture as their authority. We have found that there is a core value that covers every real-life and day-to-day situation we have faced.

Core values have allowed us to summarize the whole of Scripture in 12 easily digestible concepts. Instead of having to be armed with a specific verse for every possible circumstance of life, the core values offer easy reference to the character traits that God values, in a way that even a young child can understand. Using the core values as the basis for training, rather than simply picking and choosing from the whole of Scripture, is similar to Jesus having summed up the whole law in only two commandments (Luke 10:26-28).

Here's how we have trained our children using the core value system: the base exposure to the values occurs during our "core value lessons." Two evenings per week, I (Marc) conduct a brief lesson with the family. It doesn't take any particular advance preparation or special knowledge. I simply state the particular core value I want to emphasize and read the Bible verses that support the value. In fact, I often just read some of the verses found in this book, in the companion volume, *Values-Driven Discipleship*, or (of course) the Bible directly, to support my lessons.

We'll follow up with a simple illustration from a recent family occurrence to make it memorable, or engage in a related discussion for as long as there is interest. If one of the verses I've read readily suggests a follow-up game or activity, we will do that. Some of these games have become long-standing family favorites, like the "roaring lion" game (see 1 Peter 5:8-9).

I do two different lessons on the same core value during each week, and introduce a new core value the following week. The lessons typically take no more than 10 to 15 minutes and are usually done after dinner. These lessons offer a solid biblical foundation for observance of the core values.

In addition to the formal core value lessons, we also occasionally choose a core value "theme" for each day, which can be a great help at those times when the children need encouragement in exhibiting a certain character trait. We might provide focused activities that will emphasize a specific core value, and will be on the lookout to offer praise (and maybe even an extra little treat!) when we catch them living out the value of the day. For example, the children will go through stages when it seems they're having difficulty sharing (an expression of the core value of generosity). We'll have a "sharing" day where they'll have a certain number of chores, and they'll have to share the work cooperatively. They may also get to choose one toy or game to play with for a set period of time, all together.

Throughout the day, we also try to spontaneously reward progress and significant evidence of the core values with a small treat like a fruit snack, an extra 10 minutes of play time for our school-age children, an early release from chore time (with Mom or a sibling finishing the task), a sticker for the younger children, or something similar.

Modeling the Core Values as Biblical Precepts

Consistent core value training also means that we all strive to apply them in life's circumstances on a daily basis. It's as simple as pointing out which core value God would like to see us live by in any given situation. For example, if the children are having a hard time sharing a toy, we can say something very brief like, "Because generosity is a core value of God, he wants us to share. Who would like to be blessed by obeying God and sharing?"

Similarly, if we notice a core value playing out in our own lives, we will bring it to the children's attention. One example might be, "Well, guys, I don't like getting stuck in traffic—and I'm sure you don't either. But since 'praise' is a core value, let's praise God that maybe he's using the traffic to keep us from an accident, or to keep us in perfect timing for whatever he has planned ahead. Maybe we can put on some praise music while we wait." In this way, the children are being consistently trained in the core values and they see that living according to God's precepts is important to everyone in the household.

Benefits of the Core Value Training Method

We cannot emphasize enough that the classroom of life is where the training in God's values really occurs. The values-driven family model does not eliminate the reality of challenges. Children are children (need we say more?), and parents are merely imperfect humans. We parents will often be tested to our limits—and equally often, it seems, beyond. We find, however, that real life presents many "teachable moments" that bring the core values to life. This 18-year proving ground is where the core values travel the 12 inches from the child's mind to the child's heart.

For us, the advantages of using this method for biblical training have been many. The core values are easy to teach. They are well-supported in Scripture and therefore are true and real. This has made the process of teaching God's Word far less intimidating. As a result, *the core value training method affords the opportunity to put children's spiritual training where it belongs—in the home!*

Supporting core value training by reading from the Bible has lent a lot of authority to our "rules" and instruction. It is not just Dad or Mom saying, *do this because I said so*; it's the Word of God. Children come to have a great respect for God's Word and its ultimate authority in their lives.

Further, core value training teaches biblical precepts. It develops both a knowledge of God's Word and an obedience to it. It specifically targets the child's heart and character and provides a tangible means of living out the Scriptures, day in and day out.

The repetition, illustrations, and relevant applications help to commit the core values, and God's Word, to our children's memories. Think about it: if you focus on one core value at a time and teach two lessons on that value each week, you will teach each core value a total of four times a year. That, with repeated daily emphasis, really drives the point home. This method of training has also allowed us to reinforce certain core values on as as-needed basis: to make a particular point, to correct a behavior, or explain a major family decision.

As an added benefit, the process of core value training has also encouraged us, as parents, to abide by these biblical precepts and look for applications in everyday life. Modeling biblical living is equally easier for us as it is for our children when all we have to do is refer to that "compass" in the midst of what can be everyday chaos! Additionally, the twice-weekly lessons have offered us excellent family time and fellowship, which have been vital to maintaining family health and joy.

Interestingly enough, the core-value method addresses not only biblical training, but many of our long-term goals for our children as well, including: financial autonomy and success, the ability to perform respective roles within the family and in other relationships, ethical integrity, and emotional balance. It also promotes academic success, since it is *most* important to educate the child's heart. Educating the *mind* is much more easily accomplished when the foundation of a godly character has been laid with biblical living and scripturally based values training.

REFLECTIONS

Questions:
1. The current social emphasis on nursing on demand, child-driven schedules, and the like has effectively put the child, instead of the parent, at the center of the parent-child relationship—even from birth. How have your own attitudes and beliefs been shaped by cultural expectations or modern theories?
2. Why do you suppose that most people see biblical training as the church's responsibility, rather than that of parents (particularly fathers; see Ephesians 6:4)?

Practical Applications and *Additional Resources:*

One excellent resource that is strongly recommended as a companion to this book is *Values-Driven Discipleship: Biblical Instruction and Character Training Manual.* The spiral-bound manual empowers parents to take advantage of teachable moments and impart God's word at opportune times, allowing God's Word to be impressed upon their children's hearts. Visit www.valuesdrivenfamily.com to get a spiral-bound or e-book copy today.

For Additional Study:
Read and study Deuteronomy 6:1-9, which describes the training responsibilities of parents. Consider your family life in light of this passage and think about some things that you can do in your home to emulate this instruction.

Chapter 8: Staying on a Straight Path: *Encouragement*

Hebrews 3:13 (NIV) tells us that it is *encouragement* that keeps us following the good path that God has set before us: "encourage one another daily, as long as it is called Today, so that none of you may be hardened by sin's deceitfulness." As such, keeping our children pointed and moving in the right direction as we progress in our family journey depends a great deal upon how we encourage them in their travels. Encouragement is the second leg of that three-legged parenting stool; it is what supports our training and lends greater stability to our day-to-day family life.

Biblically, we see that encouragement helps to ensure success in a God-given mission (for example, Deuteronomy 3:28, 2 Chronicles 35:2, 2 Samuel 11:25) and also is used to keep people's hearts with the Lord (Acts 11:23, Romans 1:12, 1 Thessalonians 3:2). This necessary encouragement comes through *relationships* of fellowship and through uplifting *words*. Both of these types of encouragement are necessary accompaniments to child training.

Encouragement Through Fellowship

A loving parent-child relationship is crucial because it keeps the child's heart in tune with his parents' hearts, providing stability and bringing joy. As such a relationship is developed, the child can rest on the security of his parents' love and is assured that their discipline is for his good. This is why the Scriptures tell us not to forsake the encouragement of our children: "…we dealt with each of you as a father deals with his own children, encouraging, comforting and urging you to live lives worthy of God…" (1 Thessalonians 2:11-12).

One of the most obvious ways we've found to be an encouragement to our children is to engage in lots of displays of affection, from hugs and kisses to pats on the back, high fives, tickles, and some rough-housing with Dad.

We also try to build relationships by including the children in our necessary activities, such as housekeeping, cooking, or household and car maintenance. Not only does this enable us to model roles and living by God's values, it also makes good quality time and helps develop the positive fellowship that is necessary for our training and discipline to be most effective.

Additionally, we've made time to focus on some of the children's interests, as well as integrating them into our own daily activities. It may be as simple as reading a favorite book, singing songs together, being involved in their imaginative play for a time, or enjoying some conversation at nighttime tuck-in.

Maintaining these loving relationships with our children requires a balance between meeting our needs and the demands of our schedules and meeting the needs of the children. If we're not careful, we are prone to going to one extreme or the other—concentrating too much on what *we* have to get done, or developing a child-centric focus that fosters selfish and demanding attitudes in the children. We've seen that the art of *balance* is essential in ensuring that the emotional needs of all family members are being met, that relationships remain healthy, and that our various roles are being adequately fulfilled.

Another element of the parent-child relationship that we've been careful to pay attention to is our own expectations. As much as we want to bring our children successfully to adulthood, it has often been a challenge to balance our long-term goals with the immediate behaviors that the children exhibit. Children of every age are bound to be childish, though in reality we'd like them to be little adults. We want to temper those impulses to a degree and conform them more and more to a higher standard, yet we also have learned to let the children enjoy some amount of silliness. For example, though we encourage them to be diligent in their labor, it's equally important to us that they enjoy their work, and their childhood, which often means that they get distracted by games of one sort or another. We simply try to keep them on track in a loving way, while also making some allowances for the stage of life that they are in.

The Element of Verbal Encouragement

When we first began our parenting journey, we tried hard to nurture loving relationships with our children in the ways we have described. We knew the value of training and discipline, and were committed to biblical consistency in these areas, and we also wanted to just *love* our children. Even with these elements in place, however, we found that our children often had difficulty receiving discipline and, as a result, weren't experiencing the heart changes that we hoped for. As we sought God for a remedy to this problem, he showed us the equal importance of *verbal* encouragement—an obviously missing piece in our own parenting puzzle.

We both grew up in homes where we *knew* we were loved; our parents did their very best in every way to bring us to adulthood successfully. Yet we both also would say that we grew up in an environment that leaned toward the critical. Whether reality or simply our own perception of things, we constantly felt like we had to "measure up," and if we failed we felt a certain condemnation. This somewhat negative overtone to our family lives, however, didn't really become obvious until we prayerfully considered our own shortcomings as parents. It was then that we saw that we were perpetuating this learned pattern of parenting, and propagating a spirit of *discouragement* rather than encouragement. As a result, our best efforts in training, discipline, and even relationship-building were falling short.

Establishing positive verbal exchanges and even tones of voice were a challenge for us because of our past experiences. To help us overcome this obstacle and draw nearer to what we felt was the biblical ideal, we designed a system for encouragement that would help us to focus on our children's progress in the faith rather than on their deficiencies (whether real or perceived). Our system has proven extremely effective, for us, at both conditioning proper behaviors *and* helping to maintain an uplifting atmosphere. We track how our children are living out the core values that we teach, train, and model, and reward their progress in faithfully following God's precepts.

Training children proactively takes diligence, and, in our opinion, requires such a system of rewards for positive encouragement. Remember, the Israelites (under law) were given rewards and punishment. The promised reward of God's blessing was designed to gain their willing obedience. In fact, God offered the rewards first, and presented the punishments only as the alternative if they disobeyed. God operated under the premise of the "carrot and the stick." We parents can follow God's example by providing a system of goal setting and rewards to encourage our children in obedience to his Word.

Encouraging Through Core Value Progress

Even if your background doesn't present you with the same challenges that we faced, certainly we all have times where the "daily grind" of parenting takes its toll, and an encouragement system may be just what is needed to maintain stability and help children and parents alike to be consistent in living out God's values. There are many viable alternatives for "behavioral charts" out there, all of which can help you accomplish this goal. However, we created our system so that it meshed with, and emphasized, our core value training and addressed not only behaviors but *heart attitudes*. We feel that this is a very powerful system, and one that you should consider. For your reference, we have included sample copies of the Core Value Progress Charts that we use (see Figure 1). You can copy it for your use or set up your own. We'll get to the details of how the chart works in just a bit.

The Values-Driven Family

Figure 1: Sample Core Value Progress Chart
Multiple children, once-a-day weekday use

Core Value Progress Chart

Faith	☐☐☐☐☐	☐☐☐☐☐	☐☐☐☐☐	☐☐☐☐☐	☐☐☐☐☐
Surrender	☐☐☐☐☐	☐☐☐☐☐	☐☐☐☐☐	☐☐☐☐☐	☐☐☐☐☐
Love	☐☐☐☐☐	☐☐☐☐☐	☐☐☐☐☐	☐☐☐☐☐	☐☐☐☐☐
Faithfulness	☐☐☐☐☐	☐☐☐☐☐	☐☐☐☐☐	☐☐☐☐☐	☐☐☐☐☐
Wisdom	☐☐☐☐☐	☐☐☐☐☐	☐☐☐☐☐	☐☐☐☐☐	☐☐☐☐☐
Self-Control	☐☐☐☐☐	☐☐☐☐☐	☐☐☐☐☐	☐☐☐☐☐	☐☐☐☐☐
Righteousness	☐☐☐☐☐	☐☐☐☐☐	☐☐☐☐☐	☐☐☐☐☐	☐☐☐☐☐
Holiness	☐☐☐☐☐	☐☐☐☐☐	☐☐☐☐☐	☐☐☐☐☐	☐☐☐☐☐
Humility	☐☐☐☐☐	☐☐☐☐☐	☐☐☐☐☐	☐☐☐☐☐	☐☐☐☐☐
Diligence	☐☐☐☐☐	☐☐☐☐☐	☐☐☐☐☐	☐☐☐☐☐	☐☐☐☐☐
Generosity	☐☐☐☐☐	☐☐☐☐☐	☐☐☐☐☐	☐☐☐☐☐	☐☐☐☐☐
Praise	☐☐☐☐☐	☐☐☐☐☐	☐☐☐☐☐	☐☐☐☐☐	☐☐☐☐☐

Now, on to how it works. Every week, we start with a fresh Core Value Progress Chart with the 12 core values listed on it; our "Master Chart" has room for several children's names. There is one space to record marks by each core value for each weekday. (Since this is somewhat of a labor-intensive process for multiple children, we have opted to take weekends off!) At the beginning of the week we pick behaviors associated with the core values—either behaviors that we wish to encourage or things we want the children to stop doing; these are their goals. All of the behaviors are age appropriate and are designed to expose an outward manifestation of an inner heart condition. This is not a list of chores. Instead of "cleaning your room," we monitor things like "good attitude" for surrender and "best work" for diligence. We normally stick with specific target behaviors for a length of time, for the sake of consistency, changing only if there is an obvious need.

Each evening (either during dinner or right before bed) we assess how the children have done that day and mark their charts (with either a check or an X) to show whether or not the goals were met. If they achieve 10 out of 12 core value goals, they receive a small treat, like a few fruit snacks or a soft candy or part of a cookie. For a perfect 12, they get a whole cookie. (A big deal in the Carrier household!) We can get away with what may seem a small reward because we rarely indulge in sweets. For children with a sweet tooth, an alternative may be necessary, or perhaps you will re-think your allowance of sweets and make some adjustments there. In any case, choose something small, but meaningful and desirable. Other rewards we've used: special reading time with Mom or Dad, extended bedtime, playing a favorite game, or maybe swimming or fishing at the pond with Dad—make it age appropriate and appealing.

If the children do not reach the prescribed goals, they do not receive a reward. However, we do go over the chart to give them praise for their progress, and to encourage improvement in needed areas. For any core values they've missed, we'll try to provide them with something immediate they can do to reinforce the desired behavior.

As a team-building exercise, we occasionally make the reward all-or-none. If one child doesn't make it, they all don't. We tell them this in advance and frequently remind them to encourage one another to live by God's values so that everyone will benefit.

At the end of the week, we tally up all the positive marks, and anyone who gets an average of over 10 daily gets a "Big Winner" award. The reward is usually a homemade ice cream sundae after church on Sunday. It can also be money or a special outing. The point is to make the reward significant enough to encourage the children to seek it, yet not extravagant enough to overindulge them.

Remember, the goal is to encourage them for consistency in behavior while maintaining a focus on the Lord. Ultimately, we want our children to choose to do the things that please God out of love and faithfulness to him. Our own understanding of this principle is vital so that we consistently communicate the purposes of the chart to our children. Certainly, distracting from this objective by over-emphasizing material pleasures is counter-productive.

Sample Target Behaviors for Core Value Progress Charts

Some suggestions for behaviors that you can target and track with the core value progress training method, each listed under its appropriate core value, are presented in Figure 2. Remember, this is only a sample. You will select the target behaviors that meet your own family's specific needs. You can stay with a particular behavior for a while until it is being performed consistently and change to encourage other behaviors as needs arise.

Benefits and Cautions for the Core Value Encouragement System

We have learned through use of this system that we, as parents, rarely see the big picture with our children's spiritual and ethical health. We often focus on the one negative thing they have done most recently, and fail to recognize all of the small positive things they had done for the remainder of the day. If we simply rated our children on a pass/fail basis, according to how *we* thought they did, they would receive much less encouragement than is promoted through use of the charts. This system forces us to review all the aspects of their behavior that *God values*, rather than simply things that seem good to us or make our lives convenient.

Figure 2: Sample Target Behaviors

Core Value	Target Behavior
Faith	Scripture memorization; prayer; sharing God's Word or testimony with others; speaking God's Word
Surrender	Obeying cheerfully; receiving discipline and instruction with a good attitude; proper submission to authority (teachers, parents, grandparents, etc.); respectful speech and action; willingly putting self aside to serve others
Love	Hugs and kisses; exhibiting patience and kindness; acts of service; showing compassion
Obedience/Faithfulness	Obeying right away; reading the Bible; fulfilling God's purposes (worship, discipleship, fellowship, evangelism, or ministry); living God's Word; following set rules, even in parents' absence
Wisdom	Taking care of possessions; thoughtful use of resources; life application of God's Word; seeking Godly counsel; attention to health and hygiene; management of time
Self-Control	Restraint in play; controlling habitual behaviors (thumb-sucking, nail-biting, etc.); using quiet voices; sharing attention in conversation; frugality; being quiet when necessary (at bed time, in church, during phone calls, etc.); for very young children—using the potty!
Righteousness	Doing good; honesty; integrity; being respectful to one another; servant leadership ("no bossing"); "above reproach"; treating others with dignity; respect for God's creation
Holiness	Godly relationships; wholesome speech; good manners; exhibiting modesty (clothing, speech, adornments, hairstyle); constructive use of time
Humility	Encouraging others in godliness; honoring others; no bragging; speaking well of others; putting others first; admitting wrong; willingly apologizing/seeking forgiveness; refusing to argue/quarrel
Diligence	Cheerful completion of tasks; doing "best work"; completing jobs in good time; working for the Lord; willingly helping others in work
Generosity	Sharing or taking turns; giving of possessions or time; use of talent for others; giving grace (showing forgiveness and mercy); showing hospitality; giving more than necessary; thinking of others in giving more than self; giving up "the best" to others
Praise	Expressions of thanks to others (thank you notes, verbal thanks); verbal praise to God/thanksgiving; praise through song or dance; smiling; positive speech; no whining or complaining

We have found that even when our gut instinct would say that a child was behaving poorly, the child may have scored very well on all but one or two core values. It has been a very enlightening experience for us to faithfully use this tool. It has also improved the attitudes of our children and has really encouraged better behavior on a consistent basis. Use of this system has not only helped us to be more encouraging to our children, but it has been a great encouragement to *us* as well, because it helps us keep a proper perspective on the "day-to-day" of being in the trenches of parenthood.

Use of the charts has also led us to an important observation about our children's behavior versus their heart condition. They may have what *we* would consider a very italics day—a good attitude, no arguing with their siblings, obedience to us as parents, and no administration of discipline. Yet, on many of those days, they still could fail to earn the 10 marks on their chart that would bring them the desired "reward."

We realized that although they are "performing" well, they still are not making the necessary effort that is required to live out *God's* values. They may play well independently and avoid altercations with their siblings, but they also aren't looking for opportunities to actively share or serve during those times. Although they have a good attitude, they are not expressing praise to God. Likewise, they might simply neglect to pray (as an expression of faith). These omissions affect their overall core value progress and show us that they need some "heart" encouragement to help them remain faithful in proactively living out God's Word. At these times, we lovingly remind them that living out God's precepts, and receiving the "rewards" that he promises us, takes committed and continuous effort.

An added benefit is that the charts are a concrete way to give meaning to something that would otherwise be abstract to young children—living out "the values that God values." Because we emphasize the heart of the child as much as the behavior, we are helping to bridge the gap between the law of obedience (to us as parents) and the goal of faithfulness to God's precepts.

With this system, we can also more easily monitor our children's behavioral "fruit" and see trends, making decisions and adjustments as necessary. Just one example: we saw poor performance with the younger children if they missed their naps. This led us to add, "Falling asleep right away" to the core value chart (under "self-control") for our then-four-year-old—who was very crabby if he didn't take a nap, but also greatly procrastinated in going to sleep, both at nap time and at night. Encouraging him in this way (in conjunction with as-needed disciplinary action) did bring the desired improvement.

Overall, our use of this system has had tremendous effects on our children's behavior and has truly tied up any loose ends in our parenting regimen. It has helped us all to make a more consistent effort to live by the values that God values, and to mutually encourage one another along the journey.

Remember, however, that the purpose of the system is *encouragement*. It can quickly be manipulated and simply become a parent's tool by which we can discourage (or reprimand) poor behaviors. We always keep in mind that no matter what target behaviors we choose, as we evaluate we should focus on praising our children for sincere effort and progress.

The children have responded with consistent improvements in behavior, and with stable performance over the long haul.

We earnestly believe that a training model that provides intentional verbal encouragement and tangible rewards, especially one such as this that focuses on values training and heart attitudes, is the missing piece that many households can successfully utilize to shore up their parenting systems. Whether parents know it or not, they have a system. Unfortunately, it may be (as it had been with us) that they focus great effort in training and necessary discipline, while haphazardly throwing out uplifting or even generic phrases of encouragement.

Successful parenting demands a good balance between the three elements of training, encouragement, and discipline, with *genuine* encouragement that is based on a heart relationship. The key is to be proactive, rather than allowing circumstances to drive our responses in a more reactionary manner. We have found that many infractions can be avoided simply by teaching the children biblical values through core value training. Encouraging the children to live out those values just completes the training circle, or becomes the second leg on the parenting stool.

REFLECTIONS

Questions:
1. Think about your parents' example in the area of encouragement. Do you see reflections of this model in your own parenting?
2. As you self-evaluate in the area of encouragement, are there any changes you believe God would have you make?

Practical Applications and *Additional Resources:*
For a detailed and practical treatment of the subject of maintaining a strong bond with your children, we recommend a wonderful book by Steven and Teri Maxwell entitled *Keeping Our Children's Hearts: Our Vital Priority*. It is available at www.titus2.com.

For Additional Study:
Encouragement isn't only verbal praise; it's also providing positive support and, in a biblical context, stimulating progress in faithfulness to God's precepts. Using a concordance, do a word study on *encourage* and *encouragement* to see these various definitions in action. Consider how you may apply these concepts more and more in your everyday family life.

Chapter 9: The Inevitable Bumps in the Road: *Discipline*

Proper training and encouragement for desired behaviors will have a positive net effect on children's behavior; however, when a child engages in a negative behavior, discipline *is* necessary. Discipline is the third leg of that "parenting stool"—without it, we will lack balance. In fact, the Bible says, "Discipline your children, and they will give you *happiness* and *peace of mind*" (Proverbs 29:17, NLT, italics added for emphasis). In other words, discipline is a key element in experiencing the everyday *joy* and *peace* that God has in store for us on our family journey.

Bear with us for a seemingly unrelated story about the importance of discipline in child training. When we were in college and as yet without children, we got our first two cats, a male and female from the same litter. We began asking questions of our vet and others we knew who had cats: What if they started scratching the furniture? What if we couldn't get them to use the litter box? What if they began scratching or biting people or jumping on the table during dinner?

A couple of people suggested using a water gun if the cats engaged in an undesirable behavior, but almost everyone said that cats didn't really respond to any kind of discipline, so it was pretty much "good luck" if we ended up with even-tempered animals who didn't misbehave. We realized that this could be a problem when we'd had them only a few days and suddenly they wanted to be up all night, playing—in our bedroom. We had a schedule to keep, and it didn't include being intermittently awakened throughout the night and being exhausted the next day. (This may sound all-too-familiar to many parents!)

We tried the water gun for about a week, to no avail. We got more and more tired, and the little kittens simply enjoyed their play. Marc decided to try giving the cats a brisk smack on the hindquarter if they exhibited undesirable behaviors. Even if it didn't work, at least we could say we'd explored the options and done our best. Much to our surprise, within a few days of consistent disciplining in this manner, the cats began to confine their playing to daytime hours and sleep in our bed at night. If they did get up to play, they went into the living room. They tried scratching the furniture instead of their scratching post, but we responded immediately in a like

The Values-Driven Family

manner, and the behavior ceased. This time of physical conditioning was short lived but had lasting positive effects.

To make a long story short, these were the best cats we've ever had. We showed them a great deal of affection, and they would always come to us when they were called—even when they became outdoor cats and avid hunters. They slept in our bed every night. In fact, we could put them in the spot where we wanted them, and there they would remain.

Our future cats didn't get the consistent discipline that these first ones did. We got too busy with work, then with our children, and cats never were quite the same joy or priority that our first two were. But these two cats taught us a very valuable lesson about the importance of training, encouragement, and (especially) consistent discipline in successfully raising children!

With our cats, discipline was used merely as a form of conditioning. With our human children, however, the purpose of discipline is to reach our children's hearts and give them the desire to obey us, as their parents, so that they can mature to a faithful obedience to the Lord and his Word. Our manner and methods of discipline should reflect those of our heavenly Father. The Lord's promise to David in Psalm 89 gives us a godly perspective on discipline:

> "'If his sons forsake my law and do not follow my statutes, if they violate my decrees and fail to keep my commands, I will punish their sin with the rod, their iniquity with flogging; but I will not take my love from him, nor will I ever betray my faithfulness.'" (Psalm 89:30-33)

God desires our faithful obedience to his precepts—for our own good—so he willingly punishes disobedience. However, this is done because of his great love and as a sign of his faithfulness. Likewise, love for our children (not anger, convenience, or social expectation) should motivate all of our disciplinary action. We must have a love relationship with our children if our discipline is to be effective, because the basis of God's discipline is his love for us (see, for example, Proverbs 3:12). Disciplining in love is one way that we, as parents, show our faithfulness to God.

Discipline Defined

Discipline serves as a deterrent to future misbehavior. It should give our children a desire to do right, if only to avoid punishment. Discipline, just like training and encouragement, is most successful when it is part of a proactively applied system. There are many acceptable forms of discipline that are available to parents and all of them can work with varying degrees of success, depending on the child's temperament and will power (or, level of defiance).

Part Two: The Parenting Part of the Journey

Although discipline is one area in which some may argue that there are *good, better,* and *best* methods, the Bible is not silent about what is *best*. We read, "He who spares the rod hates his son, but he who loves him is careful to discipline him" (Proverbs 13:24). Proverbs 22:15 tells us, "Folly is bound up in the heart of a child, but the rod of discipline will drive it far from him." Further, the Bible instructs us, "Do not withhold discipline from a child; if you punish him with the rod, he will not die. Punish him with the rod and save his soul from death" (Proverbs 23:13-14, see also Proverbs 29:15 and Psalm 89:32).

Clearly, God wants us to discipline our children as a means of correcting misbehavior and preventing future disobedience. Correction, when properly administered and received, brings wisdom, offers protection, guards against folly, and even promotes the salvation of our children's souls.

Some would argue that the "rod" referenced in Scripture can refer to *any* form of discipline, and certainly non-physical punishments have their place and purpose. However, a literal rod, or switch, when administered with love, self-control, and wisdom, should be viewed as a biblically supported and beneficial disciplinary tool. The goal of this discipline should not be to inflict pain, but rather establish the adult as an authority, to direct the child's attention toward his misbehavior, and to convey the message that the behavior is unacceptable.

Biblical discipline, however, is not the alpha and the omega of good parenting. In fact, we have already emphasized the greater importance of training and encouragement. Discipline, if not done in love and with a foundational love relationship with the child, will manifest little but a rebellious spirit.

We have not found much biblical guidance regarding the specific characteristics or administration of the rod in Scripture; however, an understanding of biblical precepts and a God-given wisdom can guide parents in its application, for maximum effectiveness in child training. We have benefited from the guidelines and teaching in *To Train up a Child* by Michael and Debi Pearl. They offer support and suggestions for biblical chastisement, with a clear (yet often overlooked) emphasis on the loving bonds of fellowship that are a necessary prerequisite for the success of this method. For information visit their Web site at www.nogreaterjoy.org.

No matter how you decide to apply the biblical teaching about discipline in your home, simply be wise and remember the purpose of discipline—it is administered *in love* for training in righteousness. Your injudicious or injurious use of any tool for punishment, particularly if it is used as a means of venting your own anger, is not acceptable in the sight of man, nor in the eyes of God.

On our parenting journey, we must often remind ourselves that *children are children.* As such, they act foolishly and often forget even well-established rules. However, we've sought to address their *heart condition* more than their *outward behavior* with the administration of any discipline.

A verbal reproof may be all that is needed, and if it is not received, *then* appropriate discipline is administered to encourage obedience.

Our Testimony

We now believe that using a switch is the *best* option for discipline, yet we were not always convinced of this. We read the book *To Train up a Child* when our first child was still a baby. We found its biblical wisdom on the process of child training to be invaluable; however, at that time, we denied the need for a literal "rod" in the disciplinary process. We used time-outs and other non-physical methods of discipline, except in extreme circumstances—at those times, we would spank, which seemed more humane.

We thought that manually spanking minimized the potential for physical injury and met our objective of providing a suitable discouragement of future misconduct. However, we found over time that the obedience we expected and desired was not consistently evident. We saw that as we had more children, they fed off of each other's misbehavior and would encourage each other to constantly test the limits. This was not at all due to inconsistency on our part. It was more a result of the shifting dynamics of our growing family. What seemed good enough with two children quickly became challenging with four. As a result, the atmosphere in our home was greatly affected. We found ourselves inadvertently raising our voices and growing angry when facing the challenges of increasingly uncontrolled behavior. The solution: the rod.

After just two days of re-alignment, the atmosphere and obedience were right back to where they were when we had had fewer children. Using a switch, consistently and appropriately, had delivered on all of the promises spelled out in Scripture. We now find that we rarely raise our voices any more. The application of biblical chastisement is equally rare. Faithfulness to the biblical model of discipline has accomplished our heartfelt desire to "get rid of all bitterness, rage and anger, brawling and slander, along with every form of malice" (Ephesians 4:31) in our home.

With this method of discipline, we have found that our children are more proactively (and consistently) living out the core values as monitored on their encouragement charts. They are also happier, likely because we (parents) are experiencing more joy and peace, and they reciprocate it. They are no longer yelled at or guilted into performing. They truly recognize the joy of obeying their parents and abiding by the core values.

Effective Discipline

One of the most foundational things we've realized in our disciplinary journey is that *we cannot prolong discipline if we expect immediate obedience*! We've learned from the example of others *not* to count to three; however, we *have* been guilty of rewarding a child with warnings and providing predictable escalations of tone of voice. All of these, however, condition the children to NOT obey promptly. We now find that we rarely need to administer physical discipline—and don't even have to raise our voices—if we simply administer punishment swiftly, decisively, and on the FIRST offense.

Think about it this way: what's the speed limit on the highway in your state? How fast do people usually travel? Where we live, the speed limit is 65 M.P.H., but people typically drive at least 75 M.P.H. Why? Because everyone knows that they won't get pulled over if they keep it right at that 10-M.P.H. grace. Apply this analogy to the atmosphere of your home: how fast are your children going? Is there a strictly enforced "speed limit," or have the children learned that they can press the limits and get away with just a bit more than what you'd like? Enforcing set rules and expectations, consistently, without warnings and without yelling, simply keeps things moving at a comfortable (and more peaceful) speed.

Non-Corporal Punishment

We see in Scripture that our heavenly Father exercised non-corporal punishment on occasion with his chosen people, the Israelites. In just one example, found in Numbers 14:36-38, we read of how the Israelites rebelled against God during their time in the wilderness. The people refused to enter the land and take their possession by force (as God commanded), because the bad report of the spies had caused them to lose faith.

Three distinct outcomes resulted: the spies who spread the bad report were killed, which was a swift, decisive, and forceful punishment that we would equate with use of the "rod" (and then some!); God withheld the blessing of the Promised Land for the remaining Israelites who gave heart to the bad report—we would liken this to grounding; and, to the faithful (Joshua and Caleb) God gave the blessing he promised—a clear form of encouragement for proper behavior.

This account provides just one fitting analogy to show how grounding and loss of privileges (taking something away) can be used as suitable forms of discipline, particularly as children age.

As parents, we have full authority to implement grounding and loss of privileges as appropriate punishments. In our opinion, however, when children are young, these alternatives should be used in concert with corporal punishment, to aid in meeting the objective of impressing God's precepts on our children's hearts. In practical terms, this means that if your child fails to put his bicycle away, it may make an impression if you take it away for a few days. If a child interrupts adults, give him a five-minute time out. This type of discipline can be used for less consequential behaviors or as a temporary alternative when corporal punishment cannot be administered.

Maintain some creativity and flexibility in your disciplinary arsenal so that you can best accomplish your God-given duties. Administered properly, other forms of discipline have their merits; however, God's prescribed method is *best*. Alternative punishments would ideally be a complement to, not a substitute for, biblical chastisement.

When to Adjust Your Method

Once children are old enough to fully understand and benefit from experiencing consequences for their behavior, corporal punishment should be phased out. Older children, especially teenagers, are aspiring adults preparing for emancipation; as such, they are unlikely to receive corporal punishment without becoming embittered. Administering physical punishment to an older child is an invitation to rebellion. At this stage, the focus of discipline should be loss of privileges and grounding, with an emphasis on relationships of fellowship so that children are encouraged to choose God's ways for themselves.

Avoiding Embitterment

The Bible tells us to encourage our children; likewise, we are also instructed to avoid *discouraging* them (see Colossians 3:21). The goal of discipline is for a child to experience a change of heart that prompts him to better behavior. However, improper administration of discipline, or discipline without adequate training and encouragement, may create negative feelings in a child that can frustrate our best efforts (see Ephesians 6:4). As such, we have found it important to monitor our children's heart attitudes in response to discipline, to see if embitterment is developing.

This is where we've seen the benefits of core value training. With each punishment that is applied, the child is given a brief reminder of the core value (with supporting Scriptures) that we are trying to encourage with the administration of discipline. This combination of re-training and discipline helps to put the Lord's precepts on the child's heart and reminds him of the purpose for our rebuke.

Likewise, we make sure that discipline is applied in an emotionless manner and is administered *before* we experience the frustration, bitterness, or anger that can be associated with escalating or continuous misbehavior. We also emphasize that the punishment is the *child's* responsibility, because he has made a poor choice. Ensuring this disconnect allows the child to focus on our intended *training* rather than on us as *the trainer*. This is vital, because embitterment and rebellion are usually feelings directed towards a person—particularly if there is negative enforcement or great emotion paired with the discipline.

Know your child's heart. Recognize how they are responding to the discipline and the values you are teaching. If the punishment is not resulting in the desired outcome, adjust accordingly. Sometimes children acclimate to punishment and you need to try a new approach. Don't simply turn up the heat in severity. The reality is, if they are not responding to the discipline *they are not learning from it.* Merely stepping up the punishment can embitter them. If a new approach is needed, seek God in prayer and he will give you something to work with.

It is important in all circumstances to retain an element of sympathy in our child training and in our discipline, when it becomes necessary. We must be able to minister to a child's emotions, and maintain a heart connection with our children, while also conforming their behaviors in the desired direction. At the same time, we cannot allow a child's emotions to become a tool by which they can manipulate our actions. In this regard, the art of balance becomes an essential element in effective parenting.

The Administration of Grace

We had a memorable series of events when our oldest son, Isaiah, was just six years old that taught us a great deal in the area of discipline. While fishing, he noticed that our cat was playing with the worm that was dangling from the end of his hook. He began teasing the cat into playing with it more. Before we could tell him to stop, he had hooked the cat's leg. The cat tried to run away, bringing further injury.

We've always taught the children how important it is to treat our pets with respect. We were also sure that Isaiah was adequately aware of the potential for injury with a fishing hook. We truly felt he should have known better than to engage in such folly so we came down pretty hard on the boy for his escapade, giving an immediate spanking and then grounding him from fishing and from all use of his fishing gear for a whole week.

The next morning, the children stayed with Dad while Mom went out to the store. I (Marc) took the opportunity to get some computer work done while the children ate breakfast—uneventfully, I assumed from the usual noise level and conversation. Yet later in the day, I came upon a fishing hook on the deck off of the dining room. When questioned about it, Isaiah admitted that he had snuck out of the house at breakfast and gotten the hook out of his tackle box.

Not only did he defy our punishment, but he also went behind my back to do it. To add insult to injury, I discovered that his tackle box was down on the dam by the pond—where he was forbidden to go without a life jacket, since he couldn't yet swim! I was flabbergasted, to say the least. All of this came to a head just before we were leaving for a much-anticipated family evening of Fourth of July fireworks. As a result, I decided that the most suitable punishment would be for our son to stay home with Grandpa, who was already scheduled to watch our sleeping baby and toddler while we were out. I also told Isaiah that he would be grounded to the house, except by permission, for the next two weeks.

The next morning, I was confused to find our second son's tackle box on the patio, since I remembered putting it away in the shed after fishing the day before. I asked Isaiah about it, and he confessed to sneaking out on Grandpa the night before, just to look in his brother's fishing gear. It was the allure of the forbidden fruit! I wanted to throw up my hands and give up in despair, since it seemed I was not reaching our son's heart and he was becoming more rebellious, rather than more obedient, with each punishment.

It was at this point that I sought the Lord for a solution, since our discipline wasn't having its desired effect. In fact, I realized that our son had become embittered and that things would only get worse if I didn't change course. I believed that the administration of grace would have the greatest effect in restoring our relationship and in leading our son back to the Lord and his ways. There were several biblical steps that I followed in giving this grace, so that our son understood both the severity of his disobedience and its effects, as well as the desired effect of grace.

First, I explained my biblical role as a father (to train, encourage, and discipline) and our son's biblical role (receiving instruction and accepting rebuke for the purposes of training in righteousness, Proverbs 13:1, Proverbs 19:27; see also 2 Timothy 3:16).

Next, I explained that I wanted to show Isaiah *grace* in this instance, removing all of the promised punishments, because I feared that the amount or severity of the punishment had caused him to turn away from the Lord. I likened it to God removing the deserved punishment for our sins through Christ (Ephesians 2:4-5). Yet just as God's grace is given only to a repentant heart, I encouraged our son to repent for his sins (see Psalm 51:17, James 4:8-10, Luke 5:32).

Then, I admitted that I had erred in coming down so hard on Isaiah in the first place, since in retrospect the fishing hook incident was more childish ignorance than disobedience. I realized that humbling myself and admitting my own shortcomings would help our son's heart to be restored (remember Luke 6:42).

Together, Isaiah and I prayed for a heart change, seeking God to bring healing and forgiveness (Ezekiel 36:26-27). After our conversation, I believed that our son had truly repented, so I said that I would show grace and remove all punishment as a way of encouraging Isaiah to better behavior and to God's ways (Romans 5:20-6:2, 1 Corinthians 15:10). Yet, this came with a warning—that if our son's behavior did not evidence a change of heart, all of the original punishments, and then some, would apply (Hebrews 6:4-6).

We were almost surprised to find an immediate restoration in relationship and to see true evidence of a heart change in our son. We didn't mention the incident again, because the administration of grace had truly fulfilled its purpose in returning Isaiah's heart to the Lord and his precepts.

Biblically, we find that when the Israelites were under law they were given rewards for obedience and were punished for disobedience. However, even if they were promised consequences for their disobedience, God still showed them grace and often revoked their deserved punishment if they were repentant. We believe that children are equally under a type of law and should occasionally be shown grace, as a way of restoring their hearts. In fact, 1 Kings 12 (the story of Rehoboam as a young king) shows how a failure to administer grace at the appropriate time can incite rebellion.

Administering grace to your child when the need arises is not the same as throwing your hands up in the air. It means making a proactive, thoughtful decision, not simply giving up. Allowing God to show you the right circumstances and timing for showing grace, and being responsive to your child's heart attitude, is critical. Showing grace, if done properly, can successfully turn a rebellious heart back to the Lord—which is the desired result of all parental discipline. Not merely outward obedience, but guiding our children to a heart attitude of faithfulness, should be the goal of our training, encouragement, and discipline. The administration of grace can be a valuable tool when the effectiveness of discipline seems to have reached its limits.

REFLECTIONS
Questions:
1. What is your process for disciplining a child who is exhibiting inappropriate behavior? Do you escalate from a threat, to a command, to a raised voice, then a red-faced yell before resorting to spanking? Would you like to change this pattern?
2. How happy are you with your disciplinary system? Do you feel that changes are necessary? What are some of the things that may keep you trying another method? Consider your own past experiences, social expectations, fears or insecurities, and the like.

Practical Applications and *Additional Resources:*
If you are interested in pursuing a biblical method of discipline, we recommend the book *To Train up a Child* by Michael and Debi Pearl. The focus of their book is *not* on discipline but rather on *proactive training;* however, they provide excellent guidelines for biblical chastisement and also discuss the heart attitudes and behaviors that parents should evidence for maximum success in its implementation. Visit www.nogreaterjoy.org for this book as well as free informational articles that focus on child training and parent/child relationships.

For Further Study:
Using a concordance or other Bible reference tools, explore how God feels about, and administers, discipline. There are many passages referenced throughout this chapter; see also Deuteronomy 8:5-6, Hebrews 12:4-11, and the Proverbs referenced in this chapter.

PART THREE: Defining the Compass Points

"You're blessed when you stay on course, walking steadily on the road revealed by GOD. You're blessed when you follow his directions, doing your best to find him." (Psalm 119:1-2, MSG)

From the very beginning of our parenting journey we, like most parents, were concerned with doing all we could to bring our children to adulthood with a love for the Lord and everything else they would need to be successful in life. Training, encouragement, and discipline were the most obvious elements that would lend themselves to the accomplishment of this goal, so our reading, study, and effort were concentrated in those areas. The previous section is our attempt to share what we've learned in these foundational areas of parenting.

We came to a point, however, where we became frustrated with our biblical training—because, as we've said, the Bible was simply a bit too overwhelming. Certainly, we did our best to pick and choose applicable verses and stories to share with our children on a constant basis. It seemed, however, like we missed out on many of the teachable moments in life because we just didn't have the time or opportunity to look up the Scriptures that we knew were relevant. We did much praying and talking about this issue to see what could be done to firm up our child training in this area.

At about this time, my (Marc's) company was developing its *core values* in an effort to better define corporate objectives and encourage healthy growth in a team-oriented environment. These would be the *ideals* that everyone would strive for together—from upper management on down. The core values weren't exactly designed to reflect what the company *was*, but rather to provide a goal for what it hoped to *embody*.

I decided to apply the core value concept in our home. I explored the Scriptures to hear from God about *his* ideal for our lives. The values I identified through my Bible study became the goal that we all strive to reach together, as a family unit. The 12 core values have become, for us, a compass that has guided us in living out the whole of God's Word. These reference points have provided us with a ready repertoire of teachable verses and precepts that have helped bring our day-to-day biblical training alive.

Maybe the idea of training your children in the values that God values is appealing to you, either because of its comprehensive coverage of biblical precepts or because of its simplicity. Yet you may wonder, as we did at first, just *what* are you supposed to teach? What *are* these core values, exactly? In this section, we'll explore and define, one by one, each of the core values, and share with you some of what we've learned from our own biblical study and life application of God's Word.

Living out the core values is God's desire for us, since they embody the Christ-like character that he wants us to exhibit. Yet it is also important that we model the core values as an essential component of our child training. As such, each chapter will include a "For Your Children" section that offers some insight on how we, as parents, can both *model* and *teach* the core values. Our hope is to make it easier for you to help your children understand and practice the core values alongside of you.

Since the Scriptures tell us that as we live according to God's values and precepts, he is faithful to bless us (for example, Luke 11:28), each chapter will conclude with a bit of encouragement from God's Word, which hopefully will help you to persevere in following the good path that the Lord has set before you. Among the many incredible things he offers to those who obey his precepts are joy, peace, and success; these are promises that we, as faithful parents, can trust God for as we navigate the long and winding roads on our family journey.

As we have meditated upon these wonderful and true promises and experienced them first-hand, we've seen that our expectations of "blessing" aren't always what God ultimately delivers. We've found, for example, that we've at times confused worldly *happiness* with *joy*, which only comes from knowing that God is in everything and has a purpose for all of our circumstances (see, for example, Habakkuk 3:17-19). In the same way, we might seek the *security* of feeling like we have circumstances under our own control (see Job 31:24-28), whereas God gives us *peace,* or a quiet confidence that comes from knowing that we're doing what he wants us to do (Psalm 29:11). Likewise, God has showed us that *success* is not simply achieving our own goals, but rather getting where *he* wants us to go (see, for example, 1 Samuel 18:14). We've seen that as we cooperate with God's plans and purposes and live out the character traits that he values, we are given fulfilling and eternally significant rewards that cannot be compared with the things of the world.

Chapter 10: From Start to Finish by *Faith*

Faith is the most foundational of the core values, for "without faith it is impossible to please God" (Hebrews 11:6). Faith is *the start* of values-driven living because it is the prerequisite to having a personal relationship with God—an essential first step in giving ourselves to God and receiving all that he has for us. Our faith also sustains us to *the finish*—seeing his Word fulfilled in our lives.

Faith: *What is it?*

"Now faith is being sure of what we hope for and certain of what we do not see" (Hebrews 11:1). Quite simply, faith is trusting in God to fulfill his Word. It means *expecting* and *believing* that God will deliver on his promises, even when they are far from being seen.

Faith in God is not the same as *belief*. The words of the apostle James are very strong in this regard: "You believe that there is one God. Good! Even the demons believe that—and shudder" (James 2:19). The Bible tells us that from beginning to end, our faith must depend upon Jesus Christ; it is through faith that we put our trust in him alone (see Romans 1:16-18, Hebrews 12:1-3). It is God's desire that we all come to know Jesus as both our Savior and our Lord, believing that he died on the cross to take our deserved punishment for our sins (Romans 10:9).

This trust is not to be placed blindly and does not mean that we need to check our brains at the church door. I (Marc) am an analytical thinker by nature and a scientist by training; as such, I studied the Bible to ascertain its truth and to see how its teachings meshed with my academic learning. I found that salvation through Christ and the teachings of Scripture were very well supported intellectually. God allowed me to "prove" him, which strengthened my faith to believe in him for "things not seen."

As we put our trust in Jesus and know that he has purchased a place for us in heaven (Colossians 1:3-6), we can be confident that he is with us throughout each day (Hebrews 4:13-16). This faith does not mean that our life's journey will lead us along smooth paths. Instead, faith gives us the assurance that through each difficulty, we are fulfilling God's purposes and becoming more Christ-like.

Not only is God with us through trials, but in fact he will often use those adverse circumstances to build our faith and help us trust him more (James 1:2-4). We had a particularly relevant experience with this after the birth of our second son, Jonah. Specialists told us that he had a congenital defect that required immediate surgery. They gave him a 50% chance of survival and a near 100% chance that he would suffer negative, long-term health effects. In the midst of all the uncertainty, God showed us great mercy and assured us that *he* was in control. John 9:1-5 became a grounding passage for us over the next few trying days.

God not only granted us supernatural peace, but gave me (Marc) a word of encouragement that sustained us throughout this period of testing. In the end, our son was miraculously healed: surgery successfully did its part, missing organs materialized, and he was home three weeks following his birth. He has never had a side effect, ever.

Through this trial and his personal hand in our circumstances, God strengthened our faith in amazing ways. In part because of this, we can continue to trust in him throughout the lesser challenges of everyday life. Our faith constantly grows through our experiences, and we gain confidence by seeing God at work in our lives on a day-to-day basis.

Jesus promises, "Everything is possible for him who believes" (Mark 9 23). This is such a strong statement that we will all occasionally feel as though we just can't trust God like that! But we can take heart in the fact that God will move even if our faith is small (see Matthew 17:20-21, Judges 6:36-40 and chapter 7). If you falter during the day-to-day challenges of life, simply ask God to strengthen your faith, and he will do it (Mark 9:21-24, Romans 4:19-21).

Our daily faith means more than simply running and hiding in our prayer closet to wait on God. True faith will prompt us to *action*: "Show me your faith without deeds, and I will show you my faith by what I do" (James 2:18). In fact, the Bible says that our faith and our actions will work together, and that our faith is made complete by what we do (see James 2:22). In faith, we seek God for direction and trust that it is he who guides us. In faith, we trust in God's Word and believe that he will give us the knowledge, wisdom, and resources that we will need to act according to his perfect purposes.

At one point, we were struggling to believe God for many of the things that we knew he had planned for our lives. We had allowed ourselves to become rather passive in pursuit of what were certainly God-given plans, simply because we didn't see anything happening. God used our two-and-a-half year-old daughter, Rebekah, as a meaningful object lesson to teach us about the importance of putting our faith into action.

At this point, Rebekah had not yet learned to open a door, and she had a really endearing way of coming right up to a closed door and yelling, "Opee doe!" Someone always came to her aid. Yet when she was faced with the 13-step climb up the basement stairs, she would never walk to the door with the same determination. Instead, she would sit on the bottom step and scream,

"Opee doe!" over and over again. We couldn't leave the door ajar because we feared that her baby sister would crawl to it and there would be an accident, so we patiently explained that she must come up the stairs *first,* and then we would be quick to open the door when she arrived.

Despite our logical explanations and persistent encouragements, she would work herself into such a fit of tears that in the end, she was unable to do what was required for her goal to be realized.

God showed us that we can behave in a like manner when it comes to the application of our faith. We are told to "ask, seek, and knock" by going to God in prayer (Matthew 7:7-8), but all too often we cry to God from "the bottom of the stairs" and remain there—unwilling or unable to act, to let God move and do *his* part. Our faith should prompt us to action, and our prayerful reliance upon God in the process can assure us that the final outcome is his.

In order to receive the blessings associated with living out the core value of faith, commit yourself to trusting in God, as he has revealed himself through the pages of the Bible. Make the Scriptures an authority in your life, believing that they have been inspired by God. As you trust in God and in his Word throughout each day, you will experience the best life God has for you now, as you also await your eternal reward.

Faith for our Children: Modeling and Teaching

We know that the Lord wants to us to produce faithful and Christ-like offspring (Malachi 2:15); if we strive for this definition of family success, we can trust in God to accomplish it. God wants us, as parents, to *have* faith, and also to encourage our children in their own journeys of faith.

Believing prayer is an important expression of faith that we can both model and encourage in our children. As we actively pray with our children, we can also teach them about what prayer is, so that they will understand and apply it in their own lives. There are five requirements for effective prayer: *asking* (Matthew 7:9-11), *believing* (James 1:6-8), *proper motivation* (James 4:2-3), *being right with God* (1 John 3:21-22), and *praying by Jesus' authority* (John 14:14, Acts 3:16). If all these conditions are met, we can be confident that God will move on our behalf: "The prayer of a righteous man is powerful and effective" (James 5:16).

When do we pray? Quite simply, *Always!* (Ephesians 6:18). We can lift our concerns to God when we are in trouble (James 5:13) or when someone is sick (James 5:14-15). These prayers of faith are particularly important, because through them we ask God's will to be done in our lives and in the lives of others.

Our children can also be encouraged to act on their faith in everyday circumstances. It is through faith that we acquire the courage and confidence we need to live out God's plans and purposes and achieve success (see, for example, Joshua 1:6-9). Faith also helps us to stand against evil, trusting in God's protection and deliverance (Ephesians 6:14, 16). Further, faith makes us bold in sharing God's Word with others (Acts 18:9-10). As we live out these truths and share the Scriptures with our children, we will build their foundation of faith so that it carries them into an adulthood of serving the Lord.

For us, encouraging our children to have a "pray without ceasing" mentality (1 Thessalonians 5:17, KJV) is something we're still working on. We try to model constant prayer and we have twice-daily family prayer times. The children are growing in this expression of faith, slowly but surely. And what a blessing to hear our four-year-old say, "Jesus, help me pound this nail straight!" while working on a woodworking project, or our six-year-old spontaneously pray for his two-year-old sister who is sick. The investment of time and effort in modeling and training the core values is well worth the benefit of helping our children along to a mature faith in Jesus Christ.

God's Promises for Walking in Faith

Our example and biblical teaching in the area of faith are essential for our children's successful emancipation. This, of course, is an important goal for us as parents. However, the Bible tells us that *we will personally experience* God's blessing as we live a life of faith, trusting in God *daily* as we put our hope in him for *eternity*.

Joy:
"that does not mean we want to tell you exactly how to put your faith into practice. We want to work together with you so you will be full of joy as you stand firm in your faith" (2 Corinthians 1:24, NLT).

"I will continue with you so that you will grow and experience the joy of your faith" (Philippians 1:25, NLT).

Peace:
"He said to her, "Daughter, your faith has healed you. Go in peace and be freed from your suffering" (Mark 5:34).

"May the God of your hope so fill you with all joy and peace in believing [through the experience of your faith] that by the power of the Holy Spirit you may abound and be overflowing (bubbling over) with hope" (Romans 15:13, AMP).

Reward and Blessing:
"anyone who comes to him must believe that he exists and that he rewards those who earnestly seek him" (Hebrews 11:6).

"'Have faith in the LORD your God and you will be upheld; have faith in his prophets and you will be successful'" (2 Chronicles 20:20).

REFLECTIONS
Questions:
1. What are some areas in which you struggle to trust in God completely? Consider things like finances, relationships, decision-making, or even the day-to-day tasks that easily overwhelm.
2. Have there been times when you have allowed fear or insecurity to keep you from doing what you felt God wanted you to do?

Practical Applications and *Additional Resources:*
Our family was greatly blessed and emboldened to reach out for God's best after reading *Ten P's in a Pod: A Million-Mile Journal of the Arnold Pent Family*, by Arnold Pent III. This book, published by Vision Forum, documents the ministry years of the Pent family as they took their family of 10 across the country, sharing the Gospel and relying on God for provision and direction every step of the way.

For Additional Study:
Faith helps us achieve a greater spiritual peace and productivity. What circumstances in your life are most prone to cause you to worry or doubt? In your time with the Lord, ask him to build your faith in these targeted areas. Scriptures for further study: Matthew 14:22-36, Mark 9:14-29, Romans 14, and James 1:5-8.

Chapter 11: We're Really *Not* in the Driver's Seat: *Surrender*

We've likened the family journey to a road trip via car, and have said that when it comes to navigation, the husband and father is the one that God has placed in the driver's seat. While this is true, a father who wants to experience long-term family success, and receive the everyday joy, peace and blessing that accompany it, will intuitively see the necessity of being guided and driven by God and his Word—not by his own mind, will, and emotions. He, and all of the members of his family, will be committed to living *surrendered* lives, giving God ultimate control over every aspect of the family journey.

Surrender: *What is it?*

Surrender is not a popular term. It brings to mind loss, forfeit and failure—yet God asks for us to surrender ourselves to him and to his will. This means giving up our own plans so that we can live according to *his* purposes. In so doing, we maximize our potential for health and happiness as we serve the Lord. Ultimately, surrender is for our *good*.

Surrender to God requires a right understanding of, and respect for, who God is. The Bible calls this, "the fear of the Lord." It is not a *fear* that produces anxiety or dread, but rather a reverent awe. The Scriptures help us understand this foundational fear:

> "What does the LORD your God ask of you but to fear the LORD your God.....For the LORD your God is God of gods and Lord of lords, the great God, mighty and awesome....Fear the LORD your God and serve him.... he is your praise; he is your God." (Deuteronomy 10:12, 17, 20-21)

Balanced, biblical teaching on the fear of God is not as common today as it once was. There is more of an emphasis on God's love, mercy and grace, to the exclusion of a reverent awe before a holy and righteous God. However, many of the blessings of the Lord are reserved for those who fear him: "How great is your goodness, which you have stored up for those who fear you" (Psalm 31:19). The fear of the Lord is a fundamental prerequisite to receiving the wonderful blessings that God has for us.

Although we fear God, we are confident that he loves us and has our best in mind. It is important to keep a balanced perspective on the nature of God, fearing him yet also trusting in his mercy and grace. The Bible is clear that these attributes of God must remain in harmony:

> "For as high as the heavens are above the earth, so great is his *love* for *those who fear him*...As a father has compassion on his children, so the LORD has *compassion* on *those who fear him*" (Psalm 103:11, 13, with emphasis added).

God *is* a gracious God and God *is* love (1 John 4:16); however, he is equally worthy of our respect and awe. Though he disciplines us as a loving father, he still shows compassion to those who fear him, for he knows our weaknesses and frailty.

If we have a right understanding of the nature of God and are willing to subject ourselves to his good plans and purposes, the Bible says we will do our best to walk in obedience to God's Word in all things (Ecclesiastes 12:13). As a result, we will want to serve God and serve others (see Joshua 24:14, Ephesians 6:7). One way that we may do this is to pray and to give generously (Acts 10:2 is just one example). We will also be more willing to submit our human pride to God and allow him to shape us as people of peace (Matthew 5:38-42).

Surrendering ourselves to God also means having a teachable spirit that willingly receives God's training through the everyday experiences of life. This is like having the "good soil" that is described in Jesus' parable of the sower (Luke 8:1-15).

God wants our surrendered hearts; practically speaking, that means that we will submit to the worldly authorities that he has put in place over us. We are called to subject ourselves to various levels of government (1 Peter 2:13-14) and obey the laws that are instituted by our governing authorities (see Mark 12:17, Romans 13:6). Our employers also exercise authority over us, and the Lord asks us to serve them cheerfully, as if serving God himself (see Ephesians 6:5, Colossians 3:22-24, and 1 Timothy 6:1).

The Bible is clear that within the universal church (also called the "body of Christ") Jesus Christ is the reigning head and the commanding authority (Ephesians 1:20-23). We *are* subject to the leadership that is placed over us within the body of Christ; however, *everyone* in the Church must subordinate themselves to Scripture and to Christ. Acts 15:1-31 is a good illustration of the authority structure of the Church and shows the proper surrender to those authorities at various levels.

Within the home, the husband and father is the head (Genesis 3:16, Ephesians 5:22). Next to him is his wife, as a helper (Genesis 2:18). The children are subject to both parents (Ephesians 6:1). This God-ordained family structure is not a question of any of the individuals being better or worse, having more or less value, or being more or less qualified. The chain of authority within a household is just another one of God's prescribed plans.

It is his order of things, put in place to maximize effectiveness within the family.

God gave Christ as an authority over man, and man as an authority over woman—not with the intent of enslaving one to the other, but rather, with the desire to bring freedom. As we live within our God-given boundaries, we are freed from many of the burdens that, by design, belong to those who have authority over us. We have the freedom to fully appreciate a life devoid of the stresses and worries that are now outside of our domain. For both men and women, a surrendered life results in tremendous freedom and joy.

Surrender for our Children: Modeling and Teaching

If we are truly surrendered to God, he will often teach us through adversity. We will be subject to his discipline, and even punishment. At these times, it just doesn't feel good to give ourselves to God, yet Hebrews 12:11 tells us: "No discipline seems pleasant at the time, but painful. Later on, however, it produces a harvest of righteousness and peace for those who have been trained by it." This is a valuable promise for us to cling to as we surrender our lives to God, in good times and in trials. It's also important that we emphasize this truth in our child training, since it will help our children understand that our discipline is designed to help them to grow in godliness. Ultimately, they will be shaped to receive and learn from God's discipline.

Discipline can be viewed as a teaching opportunity that is designed to bring us into greater agreement with God's Word. The discipline of God is for our benefit, and surrendering to that discipline is God's desire for us. Hebrews 12:10 tells us, "Our fathers disciplined us for a little while as they thought best; but God disciplines us for our good, that we may share in his holiness." Discipline opens the way to righteousness, so it should be embraced as a necessary part of the surrendered life.

Encourage your children to approach every difficult circumstance with the question, *what is God trying to teach me?* There is a lesson in everything, if we are humble enough to ask God to reveal it to us. Sometimes those lessons are painful, yet they result in great personal growth.

Remember, however, that God only subjects us to things that are for our good and that will ultimately strengthen and equip us to fulfill his perfect plans and purposes. We can rest assured that we are subjected to trials because of God's love for us (see Proverbs 3:11, Revelation 3:19, Job 5:17-22).

While discipline is designed to shape our character, punishment can be given as a consequence for wrongdoing and as a deterrent to future misbehavior. God may allow us to experience punishment as a result of our own sin and folly.

The biblical concept of punishment does not discount the forgiveness of sins that we have through Jesus. If we have put our trust in Jesus for the forgiveness of sins, we will not have to stand before God in judgment for those sins after we die. However, there *are* examples in Scripture of people getting punished for their actions while here on earth (see, for example, 2 Samuel 12, 2 Samuel 24, Acts 5:1-11). Though we may not like the word *punishment,* it is something God may use to further his purposes in our lives.

Both in discipline and in punishment, God is willing to show grace when we are repentant and when we have learned the lesson that he was trying to teach us (see, for example, 1 Kings 8:46-51, 2 Chronicles 32:25-26). We have seen this firsthand on more than one occasion. A particularly relevant instance occurred with our almost-three-year-old daughter, Rebekah, who just didn't take to potty training as fast as her brothers had, or as successfully as we had hoped she would. I (Cindy) was becoming increasingly frustrated with her accidents, and one day we had about five in a row—a record number!

By the end of the day, I must admit that I came down pretty hard on her verbally. I knew that my response wasn't going to help things, and that I needed to simply clean up the messes and encourage her to do better next time—regardless of how many times it happened. Still, I struggled to do the right thing. Marc came home from work and laughed to himself about the line-up of what he called "underwear carcasses" draped over the drying rack behind the bathroom door. He knew God was working on me to help me respond in a Christ-like way to this personally challenging circumstance. I brought the situation to God in prayer and basically told him that I would "surrender" to the situation and trust that he was working something good out of it. I asked forgiveness for my negative reaction and committed to handling things God's way in the future. Much to my surprise, this was virtually the last series of potty accidents I had with Rebekah!

This is just one example of how the core value of surrender has manifested itself in our lives, personally. As parents, we can both teach about and model a life that is surrendered to God: learning and growing through loving discipline, and giving grace when the goal of discipline has been realized.

As we encourage our children to submit to our discipline, they should willingly do so because they have a respect for our authority. Therefore, it is important that we emphasize the biblical teachings on submission to authority, so that our children mature with a right understanding in this area.

Whether it is government leaders, spiritual leaders, or household leaders, the heads (or authorities) appointed by God are entrusted with the duty of protecting the institutions they lead. Christ is the Good Shepherd of his Church, and he protects us from Satan and sin (see John 10:11-15). Elders are under-shepherds, tasked with keeping out the "wolves" of false doctrine and maintaining unity of the body (as in 1 Peter 5:1-4). Our government offers services for safety and military for protection. Romans 13:4 tells us that our governing authorities are put in place by God *to do us good.* Even in the home, we see that the headship of a husband and father offers protection and is ordained by God (see Numbers 30:3-15). Likewise, children are instructed to submit to the authority of their parents, so that it will go well with them (Ephesians 6:1-3).

God's Promises for Being Surrendered

God wants us to commit ourselves and our lives to him, because he is worthy and he has only our good in mind. Yet the Bible also reveals that submitting ourselves to God, with a right heart, brings us blessing. Here are some of God's promises for his surrendered servants.

Joy:

WAIT and listen, everyone who is thirsty! Come to the waters; and he who has no money, come, buy and eat! Yes, come, buy [priceless, spiritual] wine and milk without money and without price [simply for the self-surrender that accepts the blessing].

Why do you spend your money for that which is not bread, and your earnings for what does not satisfy? Hearken diligently to Me, and eat what is good, and let your soul delight itself in fatness [the profuseness of spiritual joy]" (Isaiah 55:1-2, AMP)

"Serve the LORD with reverent fear, and rejoice with trembling. Submit to God's royal son, or he will become angry, and you will be destroyed in the midst of your pursuits—for his anger can flare up in an instant. But what joy for all who find protection in him!" (Psalm 2:11-12, NLT)

Peace:

"No discipline seems pleasant at the time, but painful. Later on, however, it produces a harvest of righteousness and peace for those who have been trained by it" (Hebrews 12:11)

"When the Holy Spirit controls our lives, he will produce this kind of fruit in us: love, joy, peace, patience, kindness, goodness, faithfulness, gentleness, and self-control" (Galatians 5:22-23, NLT)

Reward and Blessing:

"Submit to God and be at peace with him; in this way prosperity will come to you" (Job 22:21)

"From now on if you listen obediently to the commandments that I am commanding you today, love GOD, your God, and serve him with everything you have within you, he'll take charge of sending the rain at the right time, both autumn and spring rains, so that you'll be able to harvest your grain, your grapes, your olives. He'll make sure there's plenty of grass for your animals. You'll have plenty to eat." (Deuteronomy 11:13-15, MSG)

God asks for our willing surrender to his Word, to his plans and purposes, and to his Spirit for our own best interest and for our own blessing. Deuteronomy 4:39-40 says it beautifully: "'Acknowledge and take to heart this day that the LORD is God in heaven above and on the earth below.

There is no other. Keep his decrees and commands, which I am giving you today, so that it may go well with you and your children after you....'"

REFLECTIONS

Questions:
1. Does the phrase *the fear of the Lord* have negative connotations for you? What are some of the past experiences or teachings that prompt this response?
2. What are some areas in which you struggle to surrender yourself to God or the earthly authorities? Seek God's guidance in these areas in light of the verses presented in this chapter.

Practical Applications and *Additional Resources:*
A wonderful book by Jerry Bridges, *The Joy of Fearing God*, exposes the link between joy and reverence for our Lord. Find out how surrendering to God can bring his greatest blessing.

For Additional Study:
How "fertile" we are as Christians depends on how surrendered we are—how much we've committed to God and his Word. John 15:1-8 paints a picture of the importance of staying close to God if we are to be fruitful (compare this with the parable of the sower, Luke 8:1-15). Think about some of the areas in which you might benefit from a greater surrender to the Lord (for example, finances, attitude, ministry, etc.).

Chapter 12: Fuel for the Journey: *Love*

First Corinthians 13 is often cited as "the love chapter," and rightfully so. This passage shows how much God values our love walk; in fact, without love, none of the other core value characteristics and none of the things we "do" for the Lord amount to anything. 1 Corinthians 13:7 (NLT) tells us, "Love never gives up, never loses faith, is always hopeful, and endures through every circumstance." Love is what should fuel our family journey to its finish; it is what sustains us and helps us to persevere.

Love: *What is it?*

The Bible says that God is love (1 John 4:8) and that "we love because he first loved us" (1 John 4:19). All of our feelings and expressions of love have God's love at their foundation (1 John 4:7, 12). We are called to love God and to love others (Luke 10:27). As we grow in our intimacy with God, our love for others is simply an expression of his love within us (1 John 4:16-21).

When it comes to expressing love within the family, the Bible emphasizes the husband-wife relationship as the center of the family, from the beginning when God united the first man and woman (Genesis 2:24). With a strong marriage at its foundation, the family has a much greater capacity to endure the ongoing struggles of life. God knew that the demands of family were too much for one person to carry alone: "Though one may be overpowered, two can defend themselves. A cord of three strands is not quickly broken" (Ecclesiastes 4:12). The family with the husband as one strand, the wife as another, and God himself as the third strand forms a strong unit.

The marriage is an important foundation for the health of the family. The expression of love between husband and wife is of utmost importance, since the effects of a marriage relationship, whether positive or negative, are carried into future generations. If children lack the positive example of a loving marital relationship, there is a greater likelihood that they will have problematic or failed marriages of their own. The best way for children to learn the love, patience, forgiveness, and commitment that are necessary for proper relationships is through the example of a healthy marriage. As Titus 2:7 tells us, "In everything set them an example by doing what is good."

Three Greek words for love are *eros* (which is a romantic love), *philos* (the love of friendship), and *agape* (sacrificial love). God has created the marriage relationship in such a way that all three of these levels of love are foundational for a healthy marriage. Relationships usually begin with a physical attraction (*eros*), progress into friendship (*phileo*) and culminate in a sacrificial love relationship (*agape*). This pinnacle is the love that God has for us, as expressed in the person of Christ as he gave himself on the cross for our sins (see Romans 5:8 and Ephesians 5:1-2). This is the love God calls us to live by—in fact, it is *his* love within us. We will address some specific ways of putting *agape* into action within marriage in Part Four.

As we look for expressions of God's love within our marriages, it can be easy for one or the other marriage partner to ponder *agape* and think, "My husband (or wife) sure has a long way to go!" This is the point at which we may begin praying in earnest for God to change our spouse so that our marriage can be everything that God intends. But, don't forget, we are forever looking at the speck of dust in our brother's eye, all the while ignoring the plank in our own (see Luke 6:41-42). Lest we fall into the trap of pointing fingers, it's important for each marriage partner to simply make a commitment to doing his or her best to live the life of love that is full of God's blessing. Love is one of the core values that operates according to the law of reciprocity: if you show love, it will eventually be returned to you (see, for example, Luke 6:37-38, Galatians 6:7-8).

If you are in a difficult marital situation, be guided by God's Word, live his *agape* love, believe in his promises, and persevere. God himself gave us the covenant of marriage and the blessing of family, and he hates divorce (Malachi 2:13-16); as such, *every effort should be made to save a marriage*—for the good of the relationship, for the sake of the children, and simply to honor God and his Word.

Although the marriage relationship is central to the family, we've already seen the importance of developing strong bonds of affection and relationship between parents and children. The love of a parent for a child is similar in nature to the love that God has for us as his children. Scripturally, we see many examples of the value of children to the Lord (see, for example, Mark 10:13-16, Matthew 18:1-6, Matthew 18:10). The parable of the prodigal son (see Luke 15:11-31) aptly illustrates the love of a father for even a wayward and rebellious son.

We see also that God promises children as a great blessing to the faithful family (see, for example, Psalm 127:3-5 and Psalm 128:1-4). Children are a reward from the Lord and are to be received with great joy. We are to love them as God loves them, and as God himself loves us.

Titus 2:4 instructs women to "love their...children." The word for *love*, here, is translated from the Greek term *phileo*, showing that the love of parents for children is akin to brotherly affection. There is a difference between the *agape* love of the marriage relationship and the *phileo* love between parents and children; the biblical emphasis, overall, is certainly on the former.

In fact, this particular verse (Titus 2:4) is one of the very few (if not the only) biblical references we find on specifically *loving* our children. There is a greater emphasis, instead, on our parental *duties*: teaching and training (Proverbs 22:6, Ephesians 6:4), encouragement (1 Thessalonians 2:11-12), and discipline (Proverbs 22:15, Hebrews 12:7-11). Based on these biblical examples, we see that there are many ways to *express* the love of God to our children.

It is important that we remain sensitive to the individuality of each of our children and to how they are receiving our words, deeds, and affections. As I (Cindy) pondered the idea of love being the fuel for our family journey, the analogy called to mind a book I read several years ago, called *The Five Love Languages of Children*[1]. It was a very informative and helpful look at five different ways we can actively show love to our children. The authors likened a child's need for unconditional love to having a "love tank" that needs to remain filled.

Just as a marriage relationship takes attention and effort, so does maintaining a love relationship with our children. Each one will give and receive love in unique ways, and it is our job, as parents, to make sure that love remains strong within our family unit. Without it, all of our efforts in training, encouragement, and discipline, and all of our work in living out God's values and purposes for the family, can be rendered ineffective.

Love for our Children: Modeling and Teaching

For children, the expression of love may come easily, particularly if we model that as parents. Through our example, our children can grow up with a balanced self-love, know the love of God for all people, and show God's love to others.

Just like every other parent, we get frustrated with our children and sometimes don't respond to them in the most loving ways. We may wonder how our own failings in this area will affect our children's love walk. Yet, one particularly poignant family time spoke volumes to us about the quality of love that our children were capable of.

My (Cindy's) 85-year-old grandmother (the children's "Nana") had been in and out of hospitals and nursing homes for a couple of months, and was ultimately placed in hospice care just after Christmas when our four children were ages six, four, three, and 15 months. One evening my mother called, saying that she wanted the family to come and be with Nana, since she was not doing well. Marc and I went to the nursing home for part of that night,

---

[1] Chapman, Gary D. and Campbell, Ross. *The Five Love Languages of Children.* Moody Publishers, 1997.

and the next day returned to visit with the children. They had last seen their Nana on Christmas Eve, and even in that short period of time the change in her health and appearance was dramatic. She had lost a great deal of weight, wasn't wearing the dentures they were accustomed to seeing, and at this point was semi-conscious and was receiving oxygen.

My mother was concerned that the children wouldn't deal well emotionally with seeing their Nana this way, and even suggested that we may not want to bring them. Yet when they arrived at the nursing home, they didn't shrink back from her haggard and fragile appearance or even comment on the change in her. Instead, each of them kissed her wrinkled cheek and spent some time holding her hand or talking to her. It was a blessing to see the expression of their unconditional love.

Though children may receive our love and be able to express love to others, they may have difficulty grasping the concept of "loving God," since they cannot see or touch him. It is important, then, that in addition to all the other aspects of "love," we help our children understand *how we love God.*

Ultimately, our love for God is expressed by our obedience to his Word. Jesus told his disciples, "Whoever has my commands and obeys them, he is the one who loves me" (John 14:21; see also John 14:15). Therefore, it's important for us to spend time in the Word so that we know what it is God wants us to do. This may include personal reading, listening to Bible teachings, participating in a Bible study, or reading Bible-based books. However, there is no substitute for simply reading the Bible.

It is important, also, that we pray. We can both speak to God and hear from him in the quietness of prayer. We are admonished to "pray continually" (1 Thessalonians 5:17). A constant thought-life of prayer keeps us focused on the Lord, makes us more aware of his presence, and draws us closer to him. Isn't that what a love relationship is all about?

By encouraging the habits of Bible-reading and prayer (and obedience to the Word) in our children and guiding them in an understanding of how these actions express their love for God, we are laying the foundation for their lifetime love relationship with the Lord.

God's Promises for Walking in Love

Joy:
"You love him even though you have never seen him. Though you do not see him, you trust him; and even now you are happy with a glorious, inexpressible joy" (1 Peter 1:8, NLT)

Peace:
"May grace, mercy, and peace, which come from God our Father and from Jesus Christ his Son, be with us who live in truth and love" (2 John 1:3, NLT)

"Those who love your law have great peace and do not stumble" (Psalm 119:165)

Part Three: Defining the Compass Points

Reward and Blessing:
"Let love and faithfulness never leave you; bind them around your neck, write them on the tablet of your heart. Then you will win favor and a good name in the sight of God and man" (Proverbs 3:3-4)

"For I command you today to love the LORD your God, to walk in his ways, and to keep his commands, decrees and laws; then you will live and increase, and the LORD your God will bless you in the land you are entering to possess" (Deuteronomy 30:16)

REFLECTIONS

Questions:
1. Which of the three "loves" (*eros, phileo,* or *agape*) best describes the initial stages of your relationship with your spouse? Which reflects the love you have now? As you think about the expressions of love in your marriage, what are some areas that you can focus on to show God's love more effectively?
2. Is it easy or difficult for you to express love to your children? Are there expressions of love that are more natural than others? As you contemplate your love relationship with each of your children, think about how you might strengthen the bonds of love within your family as a whole.

For Additional Study:
Although you may be familiar with 1 Corinthians 13, re-read it and self-evaluate about how you measure up in expressing God's love to others. It may help to read a different Bible translation, or you may gain a new perspective through a more in-depth study with the help a concordance and other Bible reference materials, such as an expository dictionary.

Chapter 13: Being a Dependable Vehicle: *Faithfulness*

We are careful to keep our vehicles maintained, for the safety of the passengers and to ensure good service from the cars as we drive them. By analogy, we can think of ourselves as God's "vehicles," since the individual members of the body of Christ are the instruments through which God does his work in the world (for example, Ephesians 3:10, Acts 14:27). As such, it is important that we prove ourselves dependable; this is expressed in the core value characteristic of *faithfulness*.

Faithfulness: *What is it?*

Faithfulness is akin to being trustworthy and true. Faithful people are trusted by God, and by others, to do what is right and to walk in the truth. It may be helpful, at this point, to contrast *faithfulness* with *faith*. We saw that *faith* was, simply, the trust that we put *in God* (in his character, in his Word, etc.). Faithfulness, on the other hand, describes our trustworthiness—the heart condition and actions that allow God to trust *in us*.

One of the ways we express our faithfulness is through obedience to God's Word (see, for example, 3 John 1:3, Luke 11:28). Although the spiritual blessing of eternal life is assured based solely on our faith in Jesus Christ, the earthly blessings associated with faithfulness are contingent upon our actions—specifically, our obedience to God's Word and our desire to live out his purposes. Compare the Old Testament promises for obedience in Deuteronomy 5:16 to the New Testament teaching of Paul in Ephesians 6:2-3, and it's easy to see that the earthly blessings that were associated with the Israelites' obedience to God's precepts will still apply to those living under grace—*if* they faithfully abide by those same precepts.

It may seem legalistic, or unnecessarily strict, to insist upon obedience to God's precepts if we are no longer "slaves" to the law. Some would argue that under grace there is more freedom to do as we please; after all, our sins are forgiven through Christ. The apostle Paul addressed the fallacy of this thinking with the early Church (see Romans 5:20-6:2). Likewise, Jesus himself spoke of law versus grace in Matthew 5:17-48. In part, Jesus says,

> "'not the smallest letter, not the least stroke of a pen, will by any means disappear from the Law until everything is accomplished....[U]nless your

righteousness surpasses that of the Pharisees and the teachers of the law, you will certainly not enter the kingdom of heaven.. ...Be perfect, therefore, as your heavenly Father is perfect.'" (Matthew 5:18, 20, 48)

We see that, under grace, the bar has been raised! The standard is perfection and a pure heart. But don't despair—God knows we can't achieve this impossible goal on our own. He helps us to be faithful to his Word. He has taken away our sins through Christ *and* given us the ability to resist sin and live holy lives (see Romans 3: 21-26, Romans 8:12-14).

God wants us to obey his Word—not out of obligation, but as a sign of our faithfulness to him. As with all things, if he asks it of us, he makes his help available and gives us his grace to accomplish the task. Obedience *is* possible, and with it comes good things:

"'Now what I am commanding you today is not too difficult for you or beyond your reach... [T]he word is very near you; it is in your mouth and in your heart so you may obey it. ...I command you today...to keep his commands, decrees and laws; then you will live and increase, and the LORD your God will bless you...'" (Deuteronomy 30:11, 14, 16)

We'll say it again: *seeking God's direction is perfection*. Desiring his best and doing *our* best will ultimately result in God's best for us. We are reminded of the importance of depending upon God and his Holy Spirit in this process: "So I say, live by the Spirit.... [I]f you are led by the Spirit, you are not under law. ... Since we live by the Spirit, let us keep in step with the Spirit" (Galatians 5:16, 18, 25).

Don't beat yourself up for being imperfect—we all are! A wise person once said that there are two kinds of people in the world: sinners and saved sinners. Faith in Christ erases our sins but does not keep us from sinning. However, we are to strive towards his standard, which is perfection. We are not to take advantage of God's grace and ignore the Holy Spirit's conviction on our conscience (see Hebrews 3:12-15). Deliberate sin will certainly not result in God's best for our lives. Yet, as we faithfully seek to live holy and righteous lives out of love for God, we can trust that God himself will help us to do so.

The apostle Paul admonished the church in Ephesus, "As a prisoner for the Lord, then, I urge you to live a life worthy of the calling you have received" (Ephesians 4:1). Not only are we to be faithful to live out God's inspired Word, but we also, in faithfulness, strive to live out the individual and corporate purposes to which God calls us.

Other practical fulfillments of the call to faithful living are honoring our marriage vows (Hebrews 13:4), keeping the sabbath holy as a day of rest and worship (Genesis 2:2-3, Exodus 31:15, Exodus 23:12), and faithfully stewarding our God-given financial resources (Proverbs 3:9-10). We believe in, and have personally experienced, great blessing and even provision beyond explanation as we have tithed faithfully over the years (see in Malachi 3:10, God's promise to reciprocate for our giving).

Faithfulness for our Children: Modeling and Teaching

Not only is faithfulness an aspect of our relationship with God, but it is also one of the key attributes that is necessary for our children's emancipation. As they transfer from our care to God's authority, we would desire that they would continue to choose to do what is right, in faithfulness to God rather than out of their long-standing obedience to parental rules. As we grow in faithfulness, it is important that we develop a character of faithfulness in our children.

When our children are under our authority, we are likely to emphasize *obedience,* or the act of doing right as directed or instructed. Obedience is an expression of faithfulness under the law (recall our introductory discussion of the first and second covenants and the distinctions between the law and grace).

Faithfulness, in contrast, is where we are trying to lead our children— *through* their obedience. As they learn to obey *our* commands, we are hopefully nurturing their hearts and spirits to desire God's ways and to live out *his* core values and purposes. Prior to emancipation, if we are successful as parents, the acts of obedience will develop into the character of faithfulness.

The outward manifestations of *obedience* and *faithfulness* are the same (obedience to God and his Word); yet, the motivations are different. Under law we obey because we are trained to do so through rewards and punishments, whereas under grace we obey out of love for God and as an expression of our gratitude to him. Therefore, the terms *obedience* and *faithfulness* may be used interchangeably, depending on whether we are talking about the law (which is an obedience of the mind) or grace (which is an obedience of the heart).

Although we've already addressed *training* in detail in the first part of this book, it's important to note here that we've found proactive training (in the sense of conditioning behaviors) to be invaluable in developing obedience in our children. This conditioning to obedience easily transitions to a character of faithfulness once it can be explained and emphasized with more formal, biblical teaching.

We have seen that as our children age, we must give them "little freedoms" and provide them opportunities to grow in faithfulness. For example, when Isaiah was almost seven and Jonah was almost five, both boys had been trained in (and showed obedience to) the rules associated with safety around our pond and yard. To help them see the importance of not only obedience but a character of faithfulness, we allowed them to go hiking on our next door neighbors' trails (their first outdoor venture that was out of our direct line of sight).

We gave them very specific boundaries that were within a few hundred yards of home and they brought a walkie talkie so we could continually communicate with them. (Of course, sending them out two-by-two was a good way to ensure accountability to our instructions, as well.) We specifically encouraged them before they left that this would be a good opportunity for them to prove themselves faithful—and that their success in doing the right thing would increase their future freedoms. They not only had an immensely fun time but were met with a lot of encouragement for their faithfulness when they returned home. We made the point to connect their faithful obedience with the reward of doing something a little out of the range of normal.

Of course, this was a small thing—but they were small children. Yet, as we provide our children with these age-appropriate ways of proving their faithfulness, they will see the value of being faithful and will be increasingly prepared for the greater freedoms that come as they approach the age of emancipation.

God's Promises for Walking in Faithfulness

Joy:
"Well done, you upright (honorable, admirable) and faithful servant! You have been faithful and trustworthy over a little; I will put you in charge of much. Enter into and share the joy (the delight, the blessedness) which your master enjoys" (Matthew 25:21, AMP)

Peace:
"I listen carefully to what God the LORD is saying, for he speaks peace to his people, his faithful ones" (Psalm 85:8, NLT)

Reward and Blessing:
"A faithful man will be richly blessed" (Proverbs 28:20)

"But he who looks carefully into the faultless law, the [law] of liberty, and is faithful to it and perseveres in looking into it, being not a heedless listener who forgets but an active doer [who obeys], he shall be blessed in his doing (his life of obedience)" (James 1:25, AMP)

"This is what Hezekiah did throughout Judah, doing what was good and right and faithful before the LORD his God. In everything that he undertook in the service of God's temple and in obedience to the law and the commands, he sought his God and worked wholeheartedly. And so he prospered" (2 Chronicles 31:20-21)

REFLECTIONS

Questions:
1. Think about the various expressions of faithfulness: obedience to God's Word and his purposes, honoring your marriage vows, keeping holy the sabbath, and tithing/stewardship. Do you feel God would want you to be more faithful in any of these areas?

For Additional Study:
Faithfulness describes the very nature of God: "The LORD, the LORD, the compassionate and gracious God, slow to anger, abounding in love and faithfulness...." (Exodus 34:6). As such, *our* faithfulness is an expression of godly character. Using a concordance or other references, do a word study of *faithfulness* to learn more about this aspect of God's nature and about his desires for us in this area.

Chapter 14: *Wisdom* is Supreme

Many of the Proverbs tell us that wisdom is of great value and should be sought at all cost. The following passage is a particularly poignant reminder of some of the reasons we should seek godly wisdom:

> "Get wisdom, get understanding; do not forget my words or swerve from them.
> Do not forsake wisdom, and she will protect you; love her, and she will watch over you.
> Wisdom is supreme; therefore get wisdom. Though it cost all you have, get understanding.
> Esteem her, and she will exalt you; embrace her, and she will honor you.
> She will set a garland of grace on your head and present you with a crown of splendor.
> Listen, my son, accept what I say, and the years of your life will be many.
> I guide you in the way of wisdom and lead you along straight paths.
> When you walk, your steps will not be hampered; when you run, you will not stumble.
> Hold on to instruction, do not let it go; guard it well, for it is your life."
> (Proverbs 4: 5-13)

Clearly, the benefits of wisdom are many: it can protect us and keep us from hardship, bring us honor, and even ensure a long and prosperous life. So, just what *is* wisdom?

Wisdom: *What is it?*

When we became parents, of course we wanted to "do" family just right. We read a few recommended books and did some basic Bible study as we went along. We thought about all that we had read and heard and discussed our thoughts about each of the different perspectives and how all of the pieces went together. Finally, we applied what we had learned to our unique situation.

This simple example can help us to define wisdom. The gathering of information from any number of sources (including the Scriptures) gives us *knowledge*. Comprehending that learning can be defined as *understanding*. The Bible says that we should seek both knowledge and understanding—yet our goal in taking these two first steps is to apply what we learn; *that* is wisdom. We can apply learned information specifically to one area, or we may generalize principles more broadly; both are important.

As we seek wisdom, we will pay attention to our own experiences and apply the lessons learned; however, we should also be eager to learn from others. Learning and growing is necessary for maturing and becoming successful—and gaining understanding solely through our own failures can make for a long and painful journey. The Bible says that "there is nothing new under the sun" (Ecclesiastes 1:9); therefore, it behooves us to leverage the life lessons of others and avoid making the mistakes that have been made by many before us. The most obvious source of wisdom, however, is not man, but rather God himself.

True wisdom is a gift from the Lord; it is far superior to the wisdom of the world. The apostle Paul recognized this when he admitted, "'My message and my preaching were not with wise and persuasive words, but with a demonstration of the Spirit's power, so that your faith might not rest on men's wisdom, but on God's power'" (1 Corinthians 2:4-5). Though Paul was a learned religious scholar with knowledge of the law and great skill in reasoning and debate, he freely admitted that his human wisdom and success would have come to nothing if it were not for the power of God at work in and through him.

If we need wisdom (or want more of it), all we have to do is ask for it. James 1:5 says, "If any of you lacks wisdom, he should ask God, who gives generously to all without finding fault, and it will be given to him." Foundational to receiving the godly wisdom that brings blessing, however, is "the fear of the Lord." Psalm 111:10 is one of many verses that connects wisdom with this reverential awe and respect: "The fear of the LORD is the beginning of wisdom; all who follow his precepts have good understanding. To him belongs eternal praise" (see also Job 28:28, Proverbs 1:7, Isaiah 33:6). Knowledge of, and faithfulness to, God's Word is equally important in gaining wisdom: "The statutes of the LORD are trustworthy, making wise the simple" (Psalms 19:7, see also Psalm 119:98-100, Matthew 7:24-27).

In several of the Proverbs, Wisdom is personified, and she calls out to us to choose the blessing of her ways (for example, Proverbs 1:20-33, Proverbs 8:1-12). One reason why we want to do this is because the days are evil and we are called to make the most of every opportunity (Colossians 4:5)—not opportunities to accomplish things for ourselves, but to live out God's Word and his purposes in a way that will draw others to the Lord. Choosing godly wisdom also protects us from the deceptive allure of worldly ways and from our own folly (1 Corinthians 3:18-19, Proverbs 14:12, Proverbs 28:26).

Wisdom is evidenced by prudence, planning, and thoughtful action (see Luke 14:28-33, Proverbs 14:15, Proverbs 15:22, Proverbs 24:5-6, Isaiah 28:23-29). By wisdom we also are able to recognize the long-term consequences of our short-term decisions and can take steps to restrain our natural impulses (Proverbs 22:3, Proverbs 23:4). Financial stewardship and time management are areas of particular concern in this regard. Further, successful leadership depends on putting wisdom into action in various ways. All of these practical applications of wisdom, including some systems and tools that you may use to help you operate in wisdom, will be discussed in much greater detail in Part Four of this book.

Wisdom for our Children: Modeling and Teaching

To maintain a functional family according to God's core values and to further the accomplishment of his purposes within the church (for this generation and the next), we must strive to live a balanced life. This takes planning and demands wisdom. As we seek godly wisdom for the purposes of family balance, we are showing our children a positive example of biblical living—one that they will carry into adulthood and live out in their own families.

Bringing the practical matters of family into balance with God's purposes for the church is a challenge for any family, but it is well worth the effort. Living balanced lives brings us peace, assures us that we will be addressing all of the vital areas in their proper proportion, and protects us from the extremes that can affect us spiritually. The Amplified Bible puts it this way:

> "Be well balanced (temperate, sober of mind), be vigilant and cautious at all times; for that enemy of yours, the devil, roams around like a lion roaring [in fierce hunger], seeking someone to seize upon and devour." (1 Peter 5:8, AMP)

Seek the wisdom of balance for the good of your family and as a model to your children. Scheduling is just one way to help achieve this goal; as stated earlier, we will address the practical implementation of schedules and planners in Part Four.

Not only can we model balanced living for the benefit of our children and the good of our family, but we can also encourage our children in the application of wisdom. The Bible offers many "teachable verses" in this area:

> "A wise son heeds his father's instruction, but a mocker does not listen to rebuke." (Proverbs 13:1)

> "A man who loves wisdom brings joy to his father." (Proverbs 29:3)

See also Proverbs 19:13, Proverbs 23:15-16, and Proverbs 10:1.

Children are never too young to benefit from an understanding of wisdom. I (Cindy) saw just how much our then-four-year-old son, Jonah, had internalized when we were out driving on the highway and I had to pull over onto the shoulder to deal with one of those "childhood emergencies" in the back seat. Jonah was watching the cars speed by but didn't realize that I had pulled safely off the road. He told me quietly and politely (but matter-of-factly), "Mom, it's not very wise to stop the car in the middle of the highway." Never underestimate the effects of your teaching and training—and keep on encouraging your children to operate in godly wisdom.

God's Promises for Walking in Wisdom

Joy:
"For wisdom will enter your heart, and knowledge will fill you with joy" (Proverbs 2:10, NLT)

"God gives wisdom, knowledge, and joy to those who please him" (Ecclesiastes 2:26, NLT)

Peace:
"Blessed is the man who finds wisdom, the man who gains understanding, for she is more profitable than silver and yields better returns than gold....Her ways are pleasant ways, and all her paths are peace" Proverbs 3:13-14,17)

Reward and Blessing:
"So shall you know skillful and godly Wisdom to be thus to your life; if you find it, then shall there be a future and a reward, and your hope and expectation shall not be cut off" (Proverbs 24:14, AMP)

REFLECTIONS

Questions:
1. If simply asking for wisdom is all that is required of us to gain the countless benefits (James 1:5), what is preventing you from maximizing your potential in this area?
2. Walking in wisdom helps us to "make the most of every opportunity." What opportunities do you feel you are missing now and could benefit from if you were to seek God in this area?

For Additional Study:
Read Proverbs chapters 1 through 9 as a couple and journal all of the benefits of wisdom. You will discover numerous areas in which God wishes to richly bless you and your family.

Chapter 15: Finishing Well: The Necessity of *Self-Control*

If we think of parenting as a journey, it's obvious that it takes perseverance to reach our final destination—it's a long haul, and we're in for the duration. If we want to "finish well," self-control is a necessity, for the Bible tells us, "Self-control leads to patient endurance" (2 Peter 1:6, NLT).

Self-Control: *What is it?*

As a homemaker and full-time mother, I (Cindy) am the one who most often deals with the problematic (and repeated) behaviors that are common to children. It can be a frustrating and even overwhelming task to consistently train, encourage, and discipline with a heart that is surrendered to God and desires his ways. There are times when, despite my best intentions, I must confess that I lose my temper. On these occasions, however, I often call to mind a comment made by Joyce Meyer in her teaching series, *Shaping the Lives of Your Children*. Although I don't remember her exact words, the spirit of the teaching went something like this: you can't get *your children* under control unless you can keep *yourself* under control.

Though we will be sharing here what the Bible says about some of the "obvious" temptations that are common to humanity, there are many more frequent, and less obvious, temptations that present themselves in everyday family life: temptations to irritation, exhaustion, imprudence, anger, and other things that, if not properly controlled, can lead us into sinful responses and potentially damage our family relationships. Because there is a great deal of practical application that can encourage us to greater self-control in these areas, we will discuss them more specifically in Part Four. For now, we'll focus on some of the more general teachings in the area of self-control.

Paul reminds us, "All athletes practice strict self-control. They do it to win a prize that will fade away, but we do it for an eternal prize" (1 Corinthians 9:25, NLT). He is speaking of the reward of eternal life that is ours through Christ. Yet, as parents, we also seek a more temporal "prize": that of seeing our children successfully transitioned from our authority to God's *and* of experiencing all of the blessings associated with faithful living along the way. Self-control is a key element in achieving these goals.

Self-control, commitment, determination, willpower, and discipline are all related. These terms all describe making a conscious, intentional decision to do (or refrain from doing) something. Admittedly, self-control has acquired some negative connotations in modern society. We're encouraged, instead, to seek self-fulfillment—often to the point of harmful self-indulgence. The idea of disciplined living is generally perceived as denying oneself of entitled pleasures. The Bible teaches us, however, that the so-called "restrictions" imposed by self-control are *for our own benefit*. God increases our potential for lasting joy and success by protecting us from all the ramifications of self-indulgence. *Self-control is protection, not punishment* (see Proverbs 25:28).

In essence, being a person of self-control means that we refuse our improper human appetites and choose to be led, instead, by the Spirit of God (Galatians 6:8). Self-indulgence may bring temporary pleasures, many of which God fully intends for us to experience at the proper time and under proper circumstances. However, failure to take control of our cravings for these pleasures can result in many unfortunate and often irreversible circumstances. The Holy Spirit helps us to subject our bodies to God's will, so that we can experience the many wonderful things that come from living his way rather than our own (see Galatians 5:22-25).

The book of Proverbs offers us much sound wisdom, and it was written by King Solomon, who is often said to be the wisest man who has ever lived. Yet, in Solomon's introduction to the Proverbs, he reveals that they are not just about wisdom—the Proverbs are also written to encourage us to greater self-control:

"The proverbs of Solomon son of David, king of Israel: for attaining wisdom *and discipline*; for understanding words of insight; *for acquiring a disciplined and prudent life*" (Proverbs 1:1-3, italics added for emphasis).

These verses imply that *wisdom is the information you need to succeed*, and *self-control is the will and determination that are necessary to apply that information*.

So what are some of the areas in which we would benefit from exercising self-control? We should watch for *any* longings or appetites that are contrary to God's precepts and the leadings of the Holy Spirit; they come in many forms and flavors: "But among you there must not be even a hint of sexual immorality, or of any kind of impurity, or of greed, because these are improper for God's holy people" (Ephesians 5:3). This pretty much puts all of the obvious vices and forms of addiction on the radar: sex, pornography, drugs, alcohol, gambling, etc. However, self-control does not stop there. Some addictions are not so obvious and may possibly include sports, television, video games, music, wealth, possessions, food, and even work. These are often unsuspecting problems, and can be quite harmful to the family if left unchecked.

Many of these things are not evil in themselves; they *become* sinful only if they interfere with our personal relationship with God or with our duties as parents, spouses, employees, or servants of the Lord. For example: sex was designed by God and was meant to be pleasurable. However, it was also intended to be an intimate act reserved for marriage. Therefore, sex itself is not sin—it is *sex outside the covenant of marriage* that is to be avoided. Similarly, we can assume that it is sinful to have money or acquire possessions, yet we are told in 1 Timothy 6:10 that "the love of money is a root of all kinds of evil." Money itself is not evil—it is our desire (or greed) for it that is sin.

Marc has always had a passion for muscle cars. He purchased his first 1968 Dodge Charger when he was just 15 years old. That was the first of many cars that he has fixed up over the years. He purchased another 1968 Charger when our sons were four and two, thinking that it would be a good project car to work on with the boys as they aged. When the restoration was complete, however, he saw that his affinity for this type of car was, perhaps, unhealthy, because he began to concern himself more with preventing the boys from damaging the car than focusing on enjoying the blessing as a family. As a result, he sold the Charger and bought a less valuable model that would require years of restoration so he could share the building process with the children. We have learned that it is important to keep our passions in check so that not only will we *do* what God wants us to do, but we will *be* who God wants us to be.

When it comes to our desires, the Bible specifically cautions us to practice self-control in the area of lust, both in pre-marital relationships and in adulterous temptations (see, for example, Proverbs 2:16-19, Proverbs 5, Proverbs 23:26-28, Proverbs 6: 23-35, Proverbs 7:4-27, Matthew 5:27-30). Likewise, we should avoid pornography, because of its effects on our minds and hearts (Luke 11:34, Romans 6:13). The Scriptures also advise control over our use of potentially harmful or controlling substances (1 Samuel 1:14, Ephesians 5:18, Proverbs 20:1, Habakkuk 2:15-16, Proverbs 23: 29-35, and Proverbs 31:4-5, for example). Exercising self-control in all of these areas goes a long way in protecting our families from lasting harm.

One of the benefits of self-control is that we are freed from the consequences of our improper human desires and from the effects of sin. As a result, we will experience the blessings that come from following God and his ways. Self-control is of value because it is a sign of our cooperation with the Holy Spirit, and it is he who ultimately empowers us to resist sin and fleshly impulses. As we voluntarily control our impulses, desires, and actions, we give God's Spirit more control to work in and through us.

Self-Control *for our Children: Modeling and Teaching*

When our children are young, there are many areas in which we are wise to help them develop greater degrees of self-control, and all for their long-term benefit: in their appetites, in their social interactions, in their impulses to anger, and in the expression of their selfish desires, to name just a few. These can be addressed through our own positive example, with proactive training, by establishing reasonable rules and expectations, and by capitalizing on everyday teachable moments.

As our children age, we also have to address the inevitable allures that accompany adolescence by openly discussing their challenges and some of the ways they can be dealt with. When temptation comes, what does the Lord say we are to do? Quite simply, *run!* (see 1 Corinthians 6:18). Joseph, the son of Jacob, did this quite literally when his boss's wife tried to seduce him (see Genesis 39: 6-8, 10-12). We can follow his example and remove ourselves from compromising situations immediately.

We see in Joseph's situation, as regards sexual temptations, that there is safety in numbers; the event took place only when "none of the household servants was inside." On the other hand, other temptations, such as substance abuse, exert a greater pull when we are outnumbered by peers. The Bible warns us to choose our friends and acquaintances wisely so that these challenges to our values will be minimized (Proverbs 12:26, Proverbs 1:10-19, Proverbs 24:1, Proverbs 23:20). As parents, we should encourage our children to form healthy friendships with like-minded peers, and provide adequate supervision of peer interactions. At this point, our own relationships with our children should also be an area of focus, so that they know we are available to talk about whatever is on their minds, with love and without judgment.

At the appropriate time, we'll also want to share (with modesty, yet truth) what the Bible says about premarital sex. This is usually referred to as "sexual immorality" (see, for example, 1 Thessalonians 4:3-5). Some verses that emphasize the importance of sexual purity include 1 Corinthians 6:13b, 1 Timothy 5:1-2, Romans 13:13-14, and 1 Corinthians 5:9-11.

The Bible says that it is good for a man not to marry, so that he might be fully available for the Lord's service (1 Corinthians 7:1-2, 8-9 and 1 Corinthians 7: 36-38). Yet we are advised to marry if we are unable to control our passions. Marriage is God's design and sex is both for procreation and for our enjoyment, within the covenant of marriage. Enjoying the gift of sex within marriage helps us to guard one another from unnecessary temptations (1 Corinthians 7:1-5). Abstinence before marriage is mandatory; however, abstinence without mutual consent within marriage is not advised, because it can lead to temptation and sin.

Maybe you've heard the expression, *little kids, little problems*—and it's certainly true that as children age, there is an increasing potential for temptation and trouble. Yet if we do our part to encourage them in self-control from a young age, they will be more likely to be strong in this area when they are faced with the greater challenges of adolescence.

God's Promises for Walking in Self-Control

Joy:
Where there is no revelation, the people cast off restraint; but happy is he who keeps the law" (Proverbs 29:18)

Peace:
"Peace and mercy be upon all who walk by this rule [who discipline themselves and regulate their lives by this principle], even upon the [true] Israel of God!" (Galatians 6:16, AMP)

"If your sinful nature controls your mind, there is death. But if the Holy Spirit controls your mind, there is life and peace" (Romans 8:6, NLT)

Reward and Blessing:
"So think clearly and exercise self-control. Look forward to the special blessings that will come to you at the return of Jesus Christ" (1 Peter 1:13, NLT)

"So, my dear friends, listen carefully; those who embrace these my ways are most blessed. Mark a life of discipline and live wisely; don't squander your precious life. Blessed the man, blessed the woman, who listens to me..." (Proverbs 8:32-34a, MSG)

REFLECTIONS

Questions:
1. What are some areas in which you would like to exercise more self-control, so that God's Spirit can help you achieve greater victory? Think about your spending habits, use of TV and media, time management, and your balance between the responsibilities of work, family, ministry, and rest.

For Additional Study:
Just a few of the many areas in which self-control has great value within the family are: finances, speech, diet and exercise, time management, and emotions. We will be touching upon each of these areas more specifically in Part Four; for now, you may benefit from engaging in a personal Bible study to see what the Scriptures have to say about each of these everyday, practical challenges. Consider Luke 16:12, Proverbs 28:7, Luke 12:42, and Proverbs 29:11.

Chapter 16: Walking in His Steps: *Righteousness*

Psalm 85:10-13 (AMP) tells us:

"Mercy and loving-kindness and truth have met together; righteousness and peace have kissed each other. Truth shall spring up from the earth, and righteousness shall look down from heaven. Yes, the Lord will give what is good, and our land will yield its increase. Righteousness shall go before Him and shall make His footsteps a way in which to walk."

These verses emphasize the value of righteousness as an expression of the nature and character of God. Our walk in righteousness is not attained by our own strength or by following our own path; to the contrary, in pursuing righteousness we are merely walking in the footsteps of our heavenly Father and bringing him glory and honor.

Righteousness: *What is it?*

We are sure we're not the only people who have wanted to walk in righteousness in order to please God—but ended up going to the extreme and focusing on our own "works" of righteousness, instead. We must often remind ourselves that our true righteousness comes from our relationship with God and by faith. We can see that the manifestation of righteousness is two-fold: first, we are declared to be in "right-standing" with God when we put our trust in Jesus for the forgiveness of our sins; second, we pursue right living as an expression of Christ's life within us.

The terms "righteous" and "righteousness," as most often used in the Old Testament, refer to a process of justice and connote innocence or blamelessness. This justification before God was not given on the basis of works alone, but also on the basis of faith: "Abram believed the LORD, and he credited it to him as righteousness" (Genesis 15:6, compare to Deuteronomy 24:13, Psalm 106:30-31).

In New Testament writings, this teaching continues to be emphasized—except that at this point, God's promises have been manifested in Christ and our righteousness rests upon his death on the cross for the forgiveness of our sins (see, for example, Romans 3:21-23, Romans 5:16-18, Romans 8:10, Romans 10:4, 1 Corinthians 1:30, Galatians 2:21, Philippians 3:8-9). We stand before God without condemnation based on what Christ has done for us, not based on our own actions.

Yet our Christ-righteousness *is*, in a sense, standards-based as well. In fact, being right with God *should* prompt us to do right, out of gratitude for what he has done for us. The Holy Spirit empowers us to do so.

The writer of the book of Hebrews talks about the importance of moving beyond the elementary teachings (or "milk") of the faith and sustaining ourselves with "meat" so that we might become teachers rather than learners. This maturity is linked to an understanding and practice of righteousness:

> "a person who is living on milk isn't very far along in the Christian life and doesn't know much about doing what is right. Solid food is for those who are mature, who have trained themselves to recognize the difference between right and wrong and then do what is right" (Hebrews 5:13-14, NLT)

If we claim the righteousness of Christ, we will also seek to manifest that righteousness in our actions, by living according to God's precepts. 1 John 3:10 (AMP) expresses it this way:

> "By this it is made clear who take their nature from God and are His children and who take their nature from the devil and are his children: no one who does not practice righteousness [who does not conform to God's will in purpose, thought, and action] is of God."

Obeying God's Word will *not* result in our salvation or bring us closer to God in itself; only faith in Christ will do that. However, obeying his Word and choosing to do right *will* protect us and result in God's blessings. We choose to live by God's precepts because of our desire to please him. There can be no other motivation. This is the foundation on which we are to pursue righteous living—doing right for God.

Righteousness for our Children: Modeling and Teaching

Your entire household can rise or fall on your commitment to live right for God (see Proverbs 14:11 and Proverbs 12:7). Abraham and Noah are two biblical examples of men whose households were blessed because of their personal righteousness (Genesis 7:1, Genesis 18:19).

Be a blessing to your children: "I was young and now I am old, yet I have never seen the righteous forsaken or their children begging bread. They are always generous and lend freely; their children will be blessed" (Psalms 37:25-26). Lead your children to the true righteousness that only comes from faith in Christ—*and* pass on the earthly blessings that follow from living a life of right actions.

Though our righteousness comes through Jesus Christ, we should also teach them the importance of living righteously. Some of the things we may choose to emphasize include honesty and integrity (Proverbs 12:22, Proverbs

6:16-19, 1 Chronicles 29:17, Ephesians 4:25, Deuteronomy 23:21-23, Numbers 30:1-2) and doing good of all kinds (James 4:17, Romans 12:17-21, Galatians 6:9-10).

It is important that we model righteous living and encourage it in our children in these immoral times. Second Timothy 3:1-5 describes the condition of mankind in the last days, and we can see that people will increasingly refuse to live by the righteous standards that God values:

> "But mark this: There will be terrible times in the last days. People will be lovers of themselves, lovers of money, boastful, proud, abusive, disobedient to their parents, ungrateful, unholy, without love, unforgiving, slanderous, without self-control, brutal, not lovers of the good, treacherous, rash, conceited, lovers of pleasure rather than lovers of God--having a form of godliness but denying its power." (2 Timothy 3:1-5)

This picture of the world is scary—not because of all the evil things on that list, but because that list may hit a little too close to home. These behaviors do not reflect the deviance of the murderer and rapist; rather, we see many of the character traits that are evident in the people we work with, the people we go to school with, and even people in our own families.

We are likely living in what God called the "terrible times in the last days." We are called to stand for righteousness, particularly in the "last days," in no uncertain terms:

> "For you were once darkness, but now *you are* light in the Lord. Walk as children of light (for the fruit of the Spirit *is* in all goodness, righteousness, and truth), finding out what is acceptable to the Lord. And have no fellowship with the unfruitful works of darkness, but rather expose *them*. For it is shameful even to speak of those things which are done by them in secret." (Ephesians 5:8-12, NKJV)

Those of us who have chosen the path of God are called to put the evil deeds of our past behind us. God wants us, as individuals and as families, to persevere in his ways and to encourage one another in our pursuit of goodness, righteousness, and truth (see Hebrews 10:23-25).

God's Promises for Walking in Righteousness

Joy:

> "You love righteousness and hate wickedness; therefore God, your God, has set you above your companions by anointing you with the oil of joy" (Psalm 45:7)

> "The prospect of the righteous is joy, but the hopes of the wicked come to nothing" (Proverbs 10:28)

Peace:
"And the effect of righteousness will be peace [internal and external], and the result of righteousness will be quietness and confident trust forever" (Isaiah 32:17, AMP).

Reward and Blessing:
"He who pursues righteousness and love finds life, prosperity and honor" (Proverbs 21:21)

"I the LORD search the heart and examine the mind, to reward a man according to his conduct, according to what his deeds deserve" (Jeremiah 17:10)

REFLECTIONS

Questions:
1. Using a concordance, Bible dictionaries, or other reference tools, study the biblical uses of the words "righteous" and "righteousness" in the Old and New Testaments. Is there a distinction in the way the words are used or in their implied (or expressed) definitions?
2. Proverbs 21:21 tells us, "He who pursues righteousness and love finds life, prosperity and honor." God wants us to seek after his righteousness, which includes expressions of "right doing" that are a reflection of our "right being" in Christ. Honestly self-evaluate, and ask yourself, what are some areas in which you could improve in the practice of righteousness?

For Additional Study:
There are several Old Testament passages that promise that the sins of the fathers will be visited upon subsequent generations, yet in Ezekiel 18, we read that sin is no longer propagated in this manner. Although the eternal punishment for sin is not passed on, the sin itself (and its temporal consequences) apparently can be. Study some of the verses on this topic (Exodus 20:4-6, Exodus 34:6-8, Deuteronomy 5:8-10, Jeremiah 32:17-19, Ezekiel 18) and consider these passages in light of the biblical teachings on the importance of both self-control and righteousness (for example, Proverbs 25:28, Proverbs 5:22-23, Proverbs 3:33, Proverbs 20:7). Think about how your own growth in self-control and righteousness can have *positive* effects on future generations.

Chapter 17: Staying on the Straight and Narrow: *Holiness*

The Bible is full of references to God's holiness, and we are encouraged to mirror this holiness in our own lives:

> "Obey God because you are his children. Don't slip back into your old ways of doing evil; you didn't know any better then. But now you must be holy in everything you do, just as God—who chose you to be his children—is holy. For he himself has said, 'You must be holy because I am holy.'" (1 Peter 1:14-16, NLT)

Living a holy life means that our personal conduct grows toward perfection and our character increasingly becomes more Christ-like.

Holiness: *What is it?*

We've often laughed at the saying, "You don't become a hamburger by going to McDonalds"; perhaps you've heard something similar. Though it's amusing, it's also easy to see the point, which we can apply to the concept of holiness: while we can stick a "Jesus fish" on our cars, or attend all of the Bible studies and church services, be active in ministry, and sport a cross necklace, these superficial "doings" don't necessarily reflect our "being"—and it is *who we are* that God is more concerned about, not *what we do*.

God *does* encourage us to holy living; however, our works can't make us holy. *The Message* paraphrase of the Bible puts it this way: "If the primary root of the tree is holy, there's bound to be some holy fruit" (Romans 11:16). Holiness, much like righteousness, then, has a dual expression. In a positional sense, it means being set apart for God. Another biblical term for this is "sanctification." God sanctifies us, or makes us holy, by his grace when we put our trust in Christ and become separated from sin.

Holiness can also refer to the manifestation of this quality in our actions. 2 Corinthians 7:1 tells us, "Since we have these promises, dear friends, let us purify ourselves from everything that contaminates body and spirit, perfecting holiness out of reverence for God." It is the life of God within us that makes us holy, yet we set ourselves apart in thought, word, and deed as we strive to live holy lives that honor God.

Don't feel bad if you look different or do things differently because of your commitment to follow Jesus Christ. In fact, you should be concerned if you *don't* look different—because we are just passing through this world as Christ's ambassadors, and we are to be sanctified by his Word (John 17:14-18). We are cautioned to remember our heavenly hope and not set our hearts on this world—this is foundational to holy living (1 John 2:15-17, Colossians 3:1-2).

The Israelites were God's chosen people. He called them out from the surrounding nations and set them apart to serve him. We see that their holiness encompassed both their covenant relationship with God *and* an oppositional relationship to the peoples around them. This idea of being set apart was reflected in their actions, as they were called to avoid the customs of the other nations:

> "You must not live according to the customs of the nations I am going to drive out before you. ...You are to be holy to me because I, the LORD, am holy, and I have set you apart from the nations to be my own." (Leviticus 20:23 and 26)

God promised Israel good things, if they would just remain holy. He chose them to be his representatives on earth—the bearers of his Word and the seed of salvation. They were commanded to not be contaminated by the sinful beliefs and behaviors of the surrounding people. They were to be pure and set apart from them. God expects the same of us Christians today:

> "offer your bodies as living sacrifices, holy and pleasing to God—this is your spiritual act of worship. Do not conform any longer to the pattern of this world, but be transformed by the renewing of your mind" (Romans 12:1-2)

Holiness for our Children: Modeling and Teaching

One area in which both our modeling and direct teaching is important to our children's holiness (and our own) is in the development of personal relationships. The Bible says, "Do not be misled: 'Bad company corrupts good character'" (1 Corinthians 15:33). We should be diligent in monitoring both our own and our children's associations and encourage friendships with those who share our family's convictions and values.

Some general "teachable verses" in the area of friendships tell us to avoid the lazy brother (2 Thessalonians 3:6-7); to protect our homes from false teachers (2 John 1:10); and even to stay away from the hot-tempered and easily angered (Proverbs 22:24-25). We are also cautioned to stay away from evil-doers (Proverbs 24:1), gossips (Proverbs 20:19, 1 Timothy 5:13-14), drunkards and gluttons (Proverbs 23:20, Proverbs 20:1) and fools (Proverbs 14:7, Proverbs 23:9).

First Corinthians 5 warns us to be particularly careful to protect our fellowship within the church, but notes that if we were to guard ourselves against all of the negative influences outside the church, we "would have to leave this world" (1 Corinthians 5:10). It is true that there are many things we can't reasonably avoid. This may be what Jesus was referring to when he prayed that his followers would not be taken from the world, but rather protected from the evil one (John 17:15). This protection (both physical and spiritual) is key to keeping ourselves and our children walking with the Lord as we go about our business in the world.

Before we place ourselves or our children in worldly situations, we must assess both the benefits and the risks. Parental guidance and a strong parent/child relationship are of utmost importance in this area. If our children gravitate toward peers or external authorities and don't have a strong bond with us, we may lose them to worldly influences. Yet if we have loving fellowship with our children, these adverse situations can become a means by which our teaching and training of God's precepts will be affirmed.

I (Cindy) recently saw a good example of how important our parental role is in shaping our children toward the Lord and his ways. During our school time, we occasionally watch one of a series of science movies that almost always contain references to evolutionary or humanistic thought, mythological gods and goddesses, and the like. Yet rather than isolate our children from these ideas—and keep them from learning valuable scientific facts—I've watched several of the movies with them and have been careful to point out the philosophies that differ from ours, talking briefly after the movie about how God wants us to view things. This also has been a good opportunity to discuss the need to respect others, even if their beliefs differ from ours.

The other day when I suggested that the boys could watch one of these movies for science time, Jonah said, "Yeah, but those have false teaching in them!" He and Isaiah both said that when the parts about gods and goddesses came on the screen, "we block our ears until we think it's over." I was glad to see that they could interact with the things of the world—even things that we may not be in agreement with—yet remain set apart for the Lord. This incident showed me that our positive guidance can prepare our children to stand in holiness when exposed to worldly elements.

Ultimately, no matter how we choose to interact with the world, the Bible tells us that we should simply be more devoted to the Lord than to the things of the world; as the apostle Paul put it, we will "use the things of the world as if not engrossed in them" (1 Corinthians 7:31). We will face many challenges in putting the positional nature of holiness into concrete practice, usually because the "right" thing is contrary to social norms. As parents, we will often have to make these choices on behalf of our children, particularly in the areas of education, moral development, and worldly exposures. We will discuss many of these practical concerns more in-depth in Part Four.

God's Promises for Walking in Holiness

Joy:
"our hearts brim with joy since we've taken for our own his holy name" (Psalm 33:21, MSG)

"What joy for those you choose to bring near, those who live in your holy courts. What joys await us inside your holy Temple" (Psalm 65:4, NLT)

Peace:
"This core holy people will not do wrong. They won't lie, won't use words to flatter or seduce. Content with who they are and where they are, unanxious, they'll live at peace" (Zephaniah 3:13, MSG)

"God the Father chose you long ago, and the Spirit has made you holy. As a result, you have obeyed Jesus Christ and are cleansed by his blood. May you have more and more of God's special favor and wonderful peace" (1 Peter 1:2, NLT)

Reward and Blessing:
"Real wisdom, God's wisdom, begins with a holy life and is characterized by getting along with others. It is gentle and reasonable, overflowing with mercy and blessings" (James 3:17, MSG)

REFLECTIONS

Questions:
1. Think about your various relationships. Are there any that may be perhaps painful, but beneficial, for you to reduce your investment of time in? Are there any other potential relationships that you have not pursued that may be an encouragement and a blessing to you?

Practical Applications and *Additional Resources:*
If you are interested in exploring the concept of holiness as a joint venture between us and God, you may want to read *The Pursuit of Holiness* by Jerry Bridges.

For Additional Study:
God makes us holy through Christ; we pursue holiness by making choices that reflect his presence within us and bring him honor. Do a biblical word study of the terms *holy* and *holiness* to see how these two concepts interact, and how God shapes us in holiness to be more like him.

Chapter 18: He Must Become Greater: *Humility*

After John the Baptist had baptized Jesus and Jesus' formal ministry had begun, some of John's disciples were disturbed to find that people were leaving John to follow Jesus. In response, John said,

> "'God in heaven appoints each person's work. You yourselves know how plainly I told you that I am not the Messiah. I am here to prepare the way for him—that is all. The bride will go where the bridegroom is. A bridegroom's friend rejoices with him. I am the bridegroom's friend, and I am filled with joy at his success. He must become greater and greater, and I must become less and less.'" (John 3:27-30, NLT)

John's response typifies an attitude of humility. He knew that God had gifted him for a particular task, to be completed during a certain season of his life—and all for the glory of God, not for his own renown. He rejoiced in completing the work that God gave him to do and in giving honor to the One to whom honor was due.

Likewise, in our life's journey we do best to follow God's plans rather than our own, committing ourselves to his work and rejoicing that he will enable us to do what will glorify him. Trouble is, we all have ideas about where we're going and lists of things to do. All too often our plans are interrupted and we easily become frustrated. It is good to remember that God will always help us to do those things that are in *his* plan, and that we honor him by exhibiting a godly character in every circumstance. To be sure, this is not always easy, particularly when we are tested by the small trials of every day: potty-training accidents, persistent misbehavior, schedules out the window, computer glitches—you name it! By embracing these moments and allowing God to become greater as we focus less and less on our own selves and our own desires, we cultivate a character of humility that is of great value to God.

Humility: *What is it?*

Humility, like surrender, is a term very easily associated with weakness, and weakness is eminently undesirable. However, Scripture teaches us that it is in our weakness that God's strength and blessings are revealed (2 Corinthians 12:9-10).

A bit of perspective to drive this point home: the *only* thing that every single miracle in the Bible has is common is that there was a great *need* that required supernatural intervention. There was a "weakness," or something that man could not accomplish on his own, apart from God. When people came to the Lord with their needs, he expressed his power in meeting those needs. God wants us to be reliant on him. Even when life is smooth and appears to be under control, he wants us to be humble enough to recognize that this, too, is from him, and not from our own strength or abilities. He will not share his glory with any man—nor does he have to.

The essence of humility is being aware that apart from the Lord, we have no wisdom, no abilities, and no strength that can bring us success. We may seem to be able to work hard and achieve, or to do good and have blessings result—but if we exalt ourselves in our efforts rather than acknowledge God, these good things will not last (Psalm 39:6-7).

Humility is about recognizing our position before God, and therefore not thinking too highly of ourselves before fellow men and women: "Do not think of yourself more highly than you ought, but rather think of yourself with sober judgment, in accordance with the measure of faith God has given you" (Romans 12:3). We should guard ourselves against comparison and judgment, since God gifts and equips each one of us uniquely for his purposes (see Galatians 6:3-5, 1 Corinthians 4:6-7)

Humility means crediting God, and not ourselves, with all of our abilities, successes, and possessions. We read, "'Let him who boasts boast in the Lord.' For it is not the one who commends himself who is approved, but the one whom the Lord commends" (2 Corinthians 10:17-18). In all we do, we seek to serve God and give him all the glory for what he is able to accomplish in and through us. God has good works prepared for us to do, but it is for him alone that we ought to do it—willingly sacrificing the praise of men to give the honor to our Heavenly Father (Matthew 6:1-4).

For many, humility is a sign of weakness; however, it is better defined as *strength under proper control.* Jesus himself put this in perspective when at many points he restrained his God-given authority and power and subjected himself to the Father's will (see, for example, Luke 4:9-12, Matthew 26:52-54, John 19:9-11). God calls us to submit to his will and consider the welfare of others. He does not call us to be weak, but rather strong and humble.

Humility for our Children: Modeling and Teaching

It is easy to define humility with words, but knowing what a humble person looks like goes a long way in helping us to model this characteristic and teach it to our children as they grow in Christlikeness. Here are some of the characteristics of a humble individual: he is willing to receive a rebuke (Proverbs 29:1), he is willing to associate with those of low position

(Proverbs 16:19, Romans 12:16), he trusts in God's plans rather than his own (Proverbs 27:1), he does not brag about himself (Proverbs 27:2), and he remembers that everything he has is God given (Deuteronomy 8:11-14, 17-18).

Additionally, it is wise to teach our children of the negative consequences associated with pride, which is the polar opposite of humility (see, for example, Ezekiel 28:1-10, 2 Chronicles 26:16, 2 Chronicles 32:25, Hosea 10:13-14). Humility can bring blessing and pride can bring downfall; yet even those who are prideful can repent and receive help and deliverance (see Daniel 4:34, 1 Kings 21:29, 2 Kings 22:19, 2 Chronicles 12: 6-7, 12).

Pride is the source of many challenges in life. Imagine if we all had a job to do and just humbly served in our designated roles, subjecting ourselves to the proper authorities—we could all but eliminate conflict! However, conflict is commonplace—in marriages, with children, in the workplace, in society, and even in the church. It is to our benefit, then, to explore what God has to say about humility in relationships. In doing so, we can bring more order and peace to all areas of our lives.

Ephesians 4:2 tells us, "Be completely humble and gentle; be patient, bearing with one another in love." We are to put up with each other's differences and be patient with them. In humility, we can recognize that we are not perfect either, and seek to overlook others' foibles rather than dwelling on them. We are an imperfect breed and need each other's grace to maintain peace.

The Bible also teaches that we should be quick to listen and slow to speak (James 1:19). Instead of trying to win arguments, we should seek to understand another's point of view. If we set out to win by making our point, we have already lost in the areas of intimacy and respect.

Above all, it is important to listen to the Holy Spirit as he convicts us. We should be willing to apologize to those we have wronged or offended. We can be transparent about our weaknesses and join together in prayer. This is an act of humility, and we are advised to do it: "Therefore confess your sins to each other and pray for each other so that you may be healed" (James 5:16). The family unit will be much stronger for it, and we will earn respect and receive grace. Within the home, this is a very powerful way to strengthen family unity.

As parents, we *can* remind our children to subject themselves to our authority for the cause of peace:

> "Remind the people to be subject to rulers and authorities, to be obedient, to be ready to do whatever is good, to slander no one, to be peaceable and considerate, and to show true humility toward all men" (Titus 3:2)

However, these admonitions should be made with love, compassion, and humility, in order to keep our children's respect (Colossians 3:12). Even as we fulfill our God-given mandates and roles as parents, we are to exhibit attitudes of humility—remember the servant-leadership of Jesus. For if we lose our children's love and respect, it is extremely hard to regain it. Winning the battle is not worth losing the war. Approach everything in love, with attentive ears and a humble response.

I (Cindy) have seen the benefits of humility on more occasions than I care to admit. When I'm having a tough day and notice that I am beginning to get frustrated with the children, I usually react in one of two ways: either I start nagging (and the children develop negative attitudes in response, which simply escalates the problem), or, I make it a point to bring them all together and confess that I'm having trouble dealing with things the way God wants me to. After apologizing, I'll usually ask them to pray for me, and sometimes I'll even ask them to help me out by trying their best to be obedient (or diligent, or loving…). I find that when I choose to humble myself and seek my children's understanding and assistance in dealing with a situation, it's easier for all of us to re-set the direction of our day and be mutually encouraging. Humility helps!

God's Promises for Walking in Humility

Joy:
"The humble will see their God at work and be glad. Let all who seek God's help live in joy" (Psalm 69:32, NLT)

"The humble will be filled with fresh joy from the LORD. Those who are poor will rejoice in the Holy One of Israel" (Isaiah 29:19, NLT)

Peace:
"the meek will inherit the land and enjoy great peace" (Psalm 37:11)

"By pride comes nothing but strife" (Proverbs 13:10, NKJV)

Reward and Blessing:
"Humility and the fear of the LORD bring wealth and honor and life" (Proverbs 22:4)

"For God sets Himself against the proud (the insolent, the overbearing, the disdainful, the presumptuous, the boastful)--[and He opposes, frustrates, and defeats them], but gives grace (favor, blessing) to the humble" (1 Peter 5:5b, AMP)

REFLECTIONS

Questions:
1. The many biblical warnings against pride show us how important it is to humble ourselves before the Lord and even before others. Just one example is the well-known proverb, "Pride goes before destruction, a

haughty spirit before a fall" (Proverbs 16:18). Are there any areas in which you would benefit from submitting yourself more to the Lord?
2. Pride, or the absence of humility, is said to be the root cause of all sin. In what area of your life in which you may be struggling would you benefit from a greater experience of humility?

Practical Applications and *Additional Resources:*

We strongly recommend a little book titled *Humility* by Andrew Murray as a resource for learning more about this core value of God. In this little volume, Andrew Murray helps us to see that the source of our humility is not our sense of sinfulness, but rather our understanding of the nature of God and his amazing grace. It is only when we truly shift our focus from self to God that he is able to abundantly equip, use, and bless us—in our ministry, in our family life, in our work, and in our relationship to him. This book has the potential to change your perspective on Christian living forever.

For Additional Study:

We've already cited Jesus as a prime example of the life of humility that is of great value to God. In your personal Bible study time, also consider Moses (Numbers 12:3), Abraham (Genesis 18:27), Joshua (Joshua 5:13-15), King David (2 Samuel 7:18-19), Mary, the mother of Jesus (Luke 1:46-48), and the apostle Paul (Acts 20:19). This is just a short list of the many men and women who had a humble heart attitude toward God. As you engage in this study, consider how God honors, exalts, and rewards those who are meek in spirit.

Chapter 19: The Rewards of our Labor: *Diligence*

One day when I (Marc) came home from work I noticed a peculiar thing—my gravel driveway appeared to be in motion. Upon closer inspection, I observed countless carpenter ants moving in unison toward their destination in about a five-foot-wide swath. An entire colony was moving from its location in the woods (a couple hundred feet from our house) to a new destination (the attic of our house!). My father, who lives with us, said he had seen the ants marching since early in the morning; how I wished he'd stopped to ask them where they were going then!

These little guys moved an entire colony—eggs in tow—what would be equivalent to about ten miles walking distance for a person, all in one day! They did it methodically and efficiently. This became a very valuable object lesson and an opportunity to share with our boys the importance of hard work. The children were fascinated that the example they had witnessed was even alluded to in the Bible (see Proverbs 6:6-8). To this day, whenever they tire or complain about their labor, we simply say, "remember the ant." This is a wonderful example of the diligence that God wants to see expressed in our character as we go about our day-to-day labors.

Diligence: *What is it?*

Diligence is, quite simply, committing ourselves to accomplishing the work set before us. It is working hard, but not in our own strength and not just for our own benefit. We work with the strength God provides, and for his glory.

We are faced with all types of labor in life: work for income, property maintenance, home management, child rearing, ministry, and even the disciplines of the faith. God calls us to be diligent in all of these areas; as we are disciplined in completing our daily tasks, we will have more time to do *his* work, in ministry. Yet all of our time and talent belong to God, not just the time we commit to ministering to others' spiritual needs. Our everyday labor is as much his as is our ministry work.

Vacations and retirement are the heartfelt desires of many in the western world. Getting up for work each day feels like a curse to most people—in fact, we may assume that labor has its origins in the curse God pronounced upon Adam after the fall into sin (see Genesis 3:17-19). However, labor was not meant to be something to be disdained. The Bible says that *before* the curse Adam was placed in the Garden of Eden to work it and care for it. In fact, he had so much work that God created a helper for him—Eve. Work existed before the curse, but was made *more difficult* after man sinned.

God *worked* when he created the entire physical universe. What did he do when he was done? He looked at what he had done and saw that it was very good; he appreciated the labor of his hands (Genesis 1:1, 31). God *invented* work; in fact, he modeled work for us! Through his own example, we see that labor is not a punishment or a curse, but rather an opportunity for creativity and enjoyment.

Work is also opportunity for achievement. After all, anything worth having is worth working for. Whether it is a healthy marriage, closeness with God, a lean physique, a beautiful yard, knowledge, professional advancement, a clean home, or God-fearing children, all these things take effort—and effort equals work. God calls us to be diligent in our work so that we can prosper in all these areas of life. If we are lazy, we will reap the fruit of our laziness. If we are diligent, we will reap the fruit of our diligence. *You get out of life what you put into it!*

Likewise, we experience a God-given inner joy when we complete a large task. The value of a job well done is worth all the work we've invested. In life, we tend to formally recognize the larger achievements: graduations, anniversaries, promotions, retirements, and so on. However, if we parse life into discrete moments, we can experience the perpetual joy of creativity and achievement on a daily basis—when the lawn is mowed, dinner is on the table, the proposal is finished, the report has been sent to the client, the project is complete...whatever accomplishments we have in completing our labor. This is just one of the rewards of diligence.

Proverbs 10:22 tells us, "the blessing of the LORD brings wealth, and he adds no trouble to it." It is important to note that the emphasis of this verse is on "the Lord"; our efforts are actually futile unless we are partnering with God. We also see that we gain wealth with "no trouble." Working as for the Lord should bring us peace, rather than stress. A similar thought is expressed in Psalm 127:2: "In vain you rise early and stay up late, toiling for food to eat—for he grants sleep to those he loves." We can work as hard as we want, yet without the Lord's blessing, our efforts are in vain. On the other hand, working diligently, with the Lord as our focus, brings us peace and rest when our work is done.

If we do *our* part in remaining committed to diligent labor and being faithful to the Lord in all of our work, then we can be assured that God will do *his* part: "The horse is made ready for the day of battle, but victory rests with the LORD" (Proverbs 21:31). Our diligence enables God to bring success. If we neglect our part, he cannot do his.

Diligence for our Children: Modeling and Teaching

The most important first step in imparting the value of diligence to our children is training them in age-appropriate labor. Children can contribute to the function and cleanliness of the household to a much greater degree than many parents think. Since chores are an area of very practical application in family living, we will address this more specifically in Part Four.

As we model diligence in our labor and encourage this character trait in our children, there are many teachable verses that we can employ to help them grow the heart attitude toward work that honors God. Ephesians 6:5-7, Colossians 3:17 and 1 Corinthians 15:58 are key verses for the value of diligence.

Teaching about "the sluggard," as the antithesis of the diligent man, also helps our children to associate hard work with blessing. Proverbs 24:30-34 describes the sluggard and the poverty that comes upon him as a result of his laziness. Proverbs 26:13-16 tells us that the sluggard looks for any excuse not to work; he'd rather stay in bed. The Bible is actually full of *negative* promises for those who are not diligent in their labor (see, for example, Proverbs 20:4, Proverbs 14:23, Proverbs 19:15, Ecclesiastes 10:18, Proverbs 6:6-11, and Proverbs 12:24).

God's Promises for Walking in Diligence

Joy:
"...the LORD your God will bless you in all your harvest and in all the work of your hands, and your joy will be complete" (Deuteronomy 16:15)

"Moreover, when God gives any man wealth and possessions, and enables him to enjoy them, to accept his lot and be happy in his work—this is a gift of God" (Ecclesiastes 5:19)

Peace:
"For six days, work is to be done, but the seventh day is a Sabbath of rest, holy to the LORD" (Exodus 31:15)

Reward and Blessing:
"The sluggard craves and gets nothing, but the desires of the diligent are fully satisfied" (Proverbs 13:4)

"Watch out, so that you do not lose the prize for which we have been working so hard. Be diligent so that you will receive your full reward" (2 John 1:8, NLT)

REFLECTIONS

Questions:
1. How would you rate your own diligence in the following areas: work (whether paid labor or homemaking), parenting, relationship building (including a relationship with the Lord), and ministry?

Practical Applications and *Additional Resources:*
Deuteronomy 6:6-7 (KJV) tells us, "And these words, which I command thee this day, shall be in thine heart: And thou shalt teach them diligently unto thy children, and shalt talk of them when thou sittest in thine house, and when thou walkest by the way, and when thou liest down, and when thou risest up." Our labors as parents are to be undertaken with all diligence so that by our perseverance and hard work our faith will be transmitted to the next generation. Meditate on these verses and discuss them as a couple.

For Additional Study:
God wants us to be people of diligence in all areas, including our spiritual growth and the expression of our faith. In your Bible study time, consider the many verses in which we are exhorted to be diligent in our faith and in our ministry for the Lord. Some examples include Colossians 4:17, 2 Timothy 4:5, and Hebrews 6:11-12—but with a concordance or other reference materials you will find many others. Consider how you may add a greater element of diligence to your own faith journey.

Chapter 20: You Can't Out-Give God: *Generosity*

The Bible talks much about sowing and reaping, both in the physical sense and in the spiritual, or non-material, sense. The idea is that if we invest much, we will gain greater rewards than if we invest little (2 Corinthians 9:6). We also have a choice of *what* we sow; for example, we can sow negative words or positive ones—either way, we will reap, but we may not always like what we harvest if we do not make wise choices in planting. This is an important concept to keep in mind when it comes to expressing the character trait of generosity, which is of great value to God.

Generosity: What is it?

God is a generous God. He gave *first*: he gave us life and he gave us salvation as the gift of his love. He also gives abundantly when it comes to our abilities, our possessions, and our wealth. We reflect this aspect of God's nature as we strive to be people of generosity by liberally and lovingly giving of our time, our talent, and our financial resources.

Our possessions and wealth are not our own. We are only managers for the Lord. King David recognized this when he addressed the people and led them in praise after their generous giving for the building of the Lord's temple: "'Everything comes from you, and we have given you only what comes from your hand. ...[A]s for all this abundance that we have provided... it comes from your hand, and all of it belongs to you'" (1 Chronicles 29:14, 16). Jesus echoed this teaching in the so-called "parable of the talents" (Matthew 25:14-30), in which the servants who increased their master's investment (according to their abilities) received reward and praise, whereas the "wicked, lazy servant" who buried his talent was thrown "outside, into the darkness, where there will be weeping and gnashing of teeth."

These Scriptures emphasize that we are given wealth and abilities to accomplish God's purposes. *We possess so that we can give* (see, for example, Matthew 10:8b). God encourages us to be productive and gain wealth—not just to provide for our own needs, but also so that we can generously provide for those who lack (Ephesians 4:28).

There is an incredible inner joy associated with giving to others. There is also tremendous blessing in giving; in fact, Acts 20:35 says, "It is more blessed to give than to receive." The law of reciprocity applies to our giving—if we give, we *shall* receive. Yet God returns to us in greater abundance than we could ever give:

"'Give, and it will be given to you. A good measure, pressed down, shaken together and running over, will be poured into your lap. For with the measure you use, it will be measured to you.'" (Luke 6:38)

You Can't Out-Give God!

Ultimately, our giving (whether of time, talent, or treasure) is a reflection of our relationship with the Lord. God delights as we express generosity to one another in every way. Love, service, and giving are what true "religion" is all about (see James 1:27, James 2:15-16, 1 John 3:17, Hebrews 13:16).

God asks us to consider specific priorities in our giving. The Bible tells us that God has a heart, in particular, for the less fortunate: the poor, orphans, widows, foreigners, and prisoners. Their plight is his plight (for example, Deuteronomy 15:7-11, Deuteronomy 24:19-22, Proverbs 19:17, Matthew 25:34-46, 1 Timothy 5:3-5).

One of the many reasons God may encourage us to generous giving is because he does not want our desires for worldly wealth or the abundance of our possessions to come between us and him. This is evident in the example of a rich young man who conversed with Jesus (Luke 18:18-25). When asked to give up his possessions and give to the poor so that he could follow Jesus, the man "became very sad, because he was a man of great wealth." He ultimately chose not to follow Jesus because of his divided interests.

When it comes to things like our health, intellect, talents, and spiritual gifts, we should likewise invest these God-given resources with the intent of fulfilling his will: "Each one should use whatever gift he has received to serve others, faithfully administering God's grace in its various forms" (1 Peter 4:10).

We can abundantly give grace, because God is gracious to us. As we show favor, forgiveness, and love to all people, we reflect the nature of God and all that he has freely given to us. Certainly, it is easier to be generous with those whom we love, and with those who will be thankful for our giving. But God asks us to extend ourselves to others when it is difficult for us to do so. Because this type of generosity involves a greater sacrifice, it especially shows the heart of God and is abundantly rewarded by God himself (Luke 6:32-36).

We can also offer support and encouragement to those around us who need it. We can provide counsel (family, financial, legal, or spiritual) to help the oppressed and less fortunate break free from their circumstances (see Psalm 82:3-4, Isaiah 1:17) or give financially to help meet needs.

In whatever way God prompts us to give (whether of our time, our talents, or our treasures), all of our giving should be done out of *love*. Paul emphasizes this in the famous "love" chapter, 1 Corinthians 13: "If I give all I possess to the poor and surrender my body to the flames, but have not love, I gain nothing" (1 Corinthians 13:3). God wants our giving to come from the heart (Exodus 25:2, 2 Corinthians 9:7). God loves a cheerful giver—so give cheerfully, and in love.

If our giving is prompted by love and if our motivation is pure, we will not *expect* anything in return. We should not give just to receive (either from God or from men). Although God *does* reward the giver, it is because of our heart in giving—not because of the act itself. In our giving we are ultimately reciprocating God's gift of eternal life. Therefore, even when we do give, it is out of thankfulness for the reward we have *already* received (Luke 14:12-14, Matthew 6:2-4).

Generosity for our Children: Modeling and Teaching

No good thing will God withhold from the generous man. Not only will he be blessed, but he will leave a legacy of blessing: "[The righteous] are always generous and lend freely; their children will be blessed" (Proverbs 37:26, see also Psalm 112:4-9). Our generous giving is a valuable example to our children. As we model generosity, we can also emphasize the many Bible verses that address this concept—for example, Proverbs 11:24 and 25, Proverbs 22:9 and Proverbs 28:27.

I (Cindy) was surprised by how our examples of giving can have a significant effect on our children. One day I was preparing a "care package" of items to send to a ministry that served abused women and their children. Of course, my nosy six-year-old son was wondering what the pile of stuff was for, so as I worked I tried to explain the purpose of the ministry and their need for the various office supplies, toiletries, and baby care items.

In the midst of my activity, I noticed that Isaiah had suddenly abandoned his morning chore and I felt a moment's irritation. It immediately melted away, however, when Isaiah placed a Ziploc bag on top of my items. It contained his prized tape player and headphones—the one he had begged his grandmother for and received as a special gift—and two of his favorite "Word & Song" Bible tapes.

Immediately, I prodded him to make sure he wanted to give away things that were so special to him. His surprising response was, "Mom, I know that this ministry is for kids, and there's a kid out there that would really like my tape player. And I'm sending the first two of my Bible tapes because they are the ones that talk about Creation—and they need to know that God made them and he loves them. If I give this, maybe they will get to know Jesus!" I knew that his sincere gift of love must touch the heart of God, so I said, "Isaiah, I am sure that God will bless you for being so generous." To which he replied, "I already *am* blessed, Mom! I feel really good inside."

There is immense value in our modeling and teaching alone, but we can also train our children in the generous use of their talents, gifts and abilities by ministering together as a family. God has uniquely gifted each of us to help others, and he will even give us a desire to reach out to a particular person, group, or need. Although young children may be limited in their abilities to express generosity in ministry, you might consider "adopting" a grandparent through a local nursing home, baking and delivering cookies and homemade inspirational cards in your community, or simply showing hospitality by regularly inviting others into your home for a family-cooked meal or some uplifting fellowship (1 Peter 4:9, Hebrews 13:2, Romans 12:13). The holidays are full of opportunities as well, like doing a fund-raiser for Angel Tree or similar ministries that serve families in need.

Like pride to humility, greed is the antithesis of generosity. The generous seek to bless others, while the greedy live to benefit primarily themselves. It is crucial that we help protect our children from greed by encouraging them in the core values of generosity and praise at all times. Just as we, as adults, can become self-satisfied with our good lot, our children can do the same (see Deuteronomy 6:10-12, Deuteronomy 8:7-10).

Whenever we see signs of selfishness in our children, we redouble our efforts to bring about a heart of thanksgiving and generosity. At those times, we are forced to take a good look at the dynamics of our lifestyle and see just why our children are having difficulty expressing this character of God; usually it's because they've been overindulged in some area.

It is natural for children to want things; much like adults, they are driven by their egocentric thinking and their carnal desires. It's only to be expected. However, as parents, we try to keep these attributes in check so that they don't grow in proportion or result in over-indulged, unthankful individuals who only want more and complain when they receive anything less. We want good things to draw our children *toward* the Lord and result in generosity, rather than *away* from the Lord through greed.

God's Promises for Walking in Generosity

Joy:
"They worshiped together at the Temple each day, met in homes for the Lord's Supper, and shared their meals with great joy and generosity—all the while praising God and enjoying the goodwill of all the people" (Acts 2:46-47)

Peace:
"A generous man will prosper; he who refreshes others will himself be refreshed" (Proverbs 11:25)

Reward and Blessing:

"A generous man will himself be blessed, for he shares his food with the poor" (Proverbs 22:9)

"Give freely without begrudging it, and the LORD your God will bless you in everything you do" (Deuteronomy 15:10, NLT)

REFLECTIONS

Questions:
1. How generous are you in your financial giving? What about in your non-material giving? Is it easier for you to give of your time and abilities, or to give of your money?
2. When you give, do you have an expectation of return or a desire for acknowledgement? Do you feel that God has blessed your giving? If not, why?

For Additional Study:
Read some examples of sacrificial giving in the Scriptures (Mark 12:41-44, 2 Corinthians 8:2-5). Balance these expressions of giving with the biblical teaching of 2 Corinthians 8:11-15, which reminds us that God only expects us to give of what we have, so that there may be equality. Consider the idea of giving "in faith" as a way of placing our need for provision squarely into God's hands and showing that we trust God to reciprocate and to provide for our needs.

Chapter 21: Keeping Our Focus: *Praise*

We've finally arrived at the last of the 12 core values of God; hopefully as we have defined the values that God values and shared what we've learned, you've been consistently putting God's Word into practice in your own life and within your family. When it comes to *that* part of the journey, it's obvious that we will never truly arrive!

As we, personally, have lived and learned and grown in the traits that express godly character, we have seen that they are, by nature, interconnected. God wants us to live out *all* of the core values in concert, as the highest expression of Christlikeness. This can be a formidable task, and it's easy to want to give up—particularly when we don't see the progress we'd like.

In our quest to live out this values-driven family paradigm, I (Cindy) struggled, on many occasions, with depression. Depression is not uncommon; I think women are particularly vulnerable because of their monthly hormonal changes, as well as those related to pregnancy and nursing. It also doesn't help that we are usually the ones who are "in the trenches," experiencing the everyday challenges associated with family life. Even if you wouldn't say you're depressed, we all have those days when it just seems like there's no light at the end of the tunnel.

So where does praise fit in? Quite simply, praise is the glue that holds everything together. Praise is what shifts our focus from *us* to *God*, and from *our problems* to *his solutions*. We have seen that many of the core value expressions have an antithesis (pride and humility, generosity and greed, etc.). My experience with depression afforded us a unique opportunity to explore its flip-side, which is most certainly *praise*.

Praise: *What is it?*

For who he is and for all he has so freely given us, *God is worthy of our constant praise!* Although we have an adversary, Satan, he is a defeated foe and he is on a short leash. Nothing gets through to us without God's prior approval, and whatever *does* happen is for our good (see Luke 22:31, Job 1:12, and Job 2:6). All of the trials and challenges we face in life will benefit us in some way: "And we know that in all things God works for the good of those who love him, who have been called according to his purpose" (Romans 8:28).

Yet how do we maintain an *attitude* of praise? It sounds like we should be angels playing harps in heaven, not living through the day-to-day of stressful meetings, unending traffic, whining children, crying babies, and so on. Praise begins in the mind—it's all about attitude. If you are focusing on the right things, praise will come naturally. Let's see what it takes.

Meditate on who God is. We praise God not only for *what he does* but for *who he is*. His very being and his very nature demand our reverence and worship, which express themselves in praise. The book of Revelation and the Psalms are full of praise and worship—as should our lives be (see, for example, Revelation 4:8, 10-11, Revelation 5:12, Psalm 96:3-5, Psalm 145:2-4). Job is a wonderful example of praise in the midst of trial. Even when almost everything he had was taken away from him, he chose to praise God:

> "At this, Job got up and tore his robe and shaved his head. Then he fell to the ground in worship and said: 'Naked I came from my mother's womb, and naked I will depart. The LORD gave and the LORD has taken away; may the name of the LORD be praised.'" (Job 1:20-21)

Because God is worthy of praise, we should exalt him regardless of our circumstances. So praise him during good times (Isaiah 12:1-5) and praise him from the depths (Jonah 2:1-10). Jonah was only delivered from the belly of the big fish *after* he humbled himself and praised God. In the same way, our personal circumstances should not keep us from praising our God—because he is God and he is worthy.

Praise him for what he does. We should praise God, first and foremost, because of his nature, his power, and his love. Keep in mind, too, that he is always present and he is always at work. Looking for evidence of God helps us to more constantly praise him. Developing this "God-radar" sets our minds on him and makes it easier to shift the focus from *ourselves* to *God*.

You may not have experienced such miracles as those documented in Scripture, yet you *have* experienced the miracle of grace—and, if you look for it, you will see that
God continually pours it upon you every day. Though you may not be parting the Red Sea, chances are that God did *something* in your life. So don't look at what God *hasn't* done, praise him for what he *has* done.

Praise God for his presence: When the challenges in life are beyond what we can bear, we must remember that though we may lose everything in this world, *nothing* can separate us from God and his love (Romans 8:31-39). His constant presence should fill us with reasons to praise.

He is and will always be with those who put their trust in him. Even when his trials were at their worst, the apostle Paul fixed his eyes on Jesus and was able to praise God through the great persecution he faced (2 Corinthians 4:8-9, 16). Likewise, if we focus on God and on the eternal, we will overcome. There is no greater illustration of this than in the person of Jesus Christ. Psalm 22:1-31 is referred to as "the song of the cross" because it prophesied the events that occurred during the crucifixion of Christ. You may also recognize that Jesus uttered the opening words of this Psalm when he was on the cross. Words of praise still are found in this song of great trial:

> "I will declare your name to my brothers; in the congregation I will praise you. You who fear the LORD, praise him! All you descendants of Jacob, honor him! Revere him, all you descendants of Israel!" (Psalm 22:22-23)

We praise God because he never leaves us, even in times of trouble.

Keep an eternal perspective. An attitude of praise becomes easier to adopt if we are looking at life from God's (eternal) perspective rather than our own limited understanding.

The apostle Paul constantly chose to focus not on his temporary trials but on what Christ had already done for him. We do well to follow his example. Romans 5:11 instructs us to be filled with joy because of our salvation: "we also rejoice in God through our Lord Jesus Christ, through whom we have now received reconciliation." We have been given eternal security. No other gift can compare. Forever praise God for this gift! Psalm 103:2-5 is another wonderful meditation to help us keep this eternal perspective.

An eternal focus means meditating on the reality of our salvation in such a tangible way that we come to realize that whether we live or die, we belong to the Lord and were made to worship and honor him (Philippians 1:20-26, 2 Corinthians 5:6-9). God is with us in life, and we will be with him in death—how awesome a thought that is!

Keep positive. God has given us salvation—never belittle the significance of this gift. Yet also consider your health, your abilities, your skills, your possessions, your loved ones, your church, your country—all of these things are precious and should not be overlooked. Dwell on what you have, not on what you don't have. View the glass as half full, not half empty. This is the power of positive thinking, and a foundation for praise.

No matter how bad things look, there is always a bright side! Take Hezekiah, for example; he received a word from God that all would be lost and his descendants would suffer. His conclusion: *"At least I won't be around to see it"* (see 2 Kings 20:16-19). *That* is some real positive thinking! Putting a positive spin on even negative situations helps us to praise God even when things seem bleak.

We also see this concept illustrated in the book of Ezra, as we read how the Israelites were strongly divided in their reaction to the rebuilding of the temple (Ezra 3:11-13). The same event brought tears to some and joy to others—their reactions were all a matter of perspective. The older men focused on the glory of the former temple and felt that the new foundation did not meet their expectations. The younger generation, however, praised God for what they *did* have, since they had not known of the former things.

The glass was half full for the youth, while it was half empty for the aged. Whatever life brings to you, receive God's blessings with praise, and you will find joy.

Forget about the past. The passage just cited (Ezra 3:11-13) reveals another important element of praise. The elders were focused on *the past.* The young people, on the other hand, were celebrating what had been accomplished in the present. Focus on *today,* and on the future, instead of remaining trapped in the past. The past is irrevocable, but with directed action and a right attitude, you *can* change the future. Isaiah 43:18-19 gives us sound instruction: "'Forget the former things; do not dwell on the past. See, I am doing a new thing! Now it springs up; do you not perceive it? I am making a way in the desert and streams in the wasteland.'" *God's best for your life is not in your past; it is in your future!*

It can be difficult to praise God in hard times, but the right heart attitude is key to receiving his best and being redeemed from our distress. Yet, we must equally guard our hearts against complacency by praising God when things are good (1 Kings 5:4-5). If the gifts he has given do not result in praise and in our desire to draw near to him, he will do what is necessary to bring us back to him—even bringing adverse circumstances into our lives (Hosea 13:6-7).

Praise for our Children: Modeling and Teaching

We can model a heart attitude of praise by genuinely speaking positive confessions from God's Word, even in difficult situations (Philippians 4:8-9), as well as by expressing thanksgiving and enjoying God for who he is (1Thessalonians 5:16). We can also encourage hearts of praise in our children by doing simple things like smiling—even when we don't feel like it (Proverbs 15:30).

Praise also comes more naturally when we are focused on others and on God more than on ourselves. We can encourage our children in a more outward-oriented perspective by rejoicing in others' success (Matthew 20:1-15), praising God for the salvation of the lost (Luke 15:4-7, Luke 15:11-32), and by worshiping corporately within the body of Christ (Acts 2:47, Ephesians 5:19-20, 1 Corinthians 14:26).

God's Promises for Walking in Praise

Joy:
"My lips will shout for joy when I sing praise to you— I, whom you have redeemed" (Psalm 71:23)

Peace:
"And let the peace (soul harmony which comes) from Christ rule (act as umpire continually) in your hearts [deciding and settling with finality all questions that

arise in your minds, in that peaceful state] to which as [members of Christ's] one body you were also called [to live]. And be thankful (appreciative), [giving praise to God always]" (Colossians 3:15 AMP)

Reward and Blessing:
"'Then this city will bring me renown, joy, praise and honor before all nations on earth that hear of all the good things I do for it; and they will be in awe and will tremble at the abundant prosperity and peace I provide for it.'" (Jeremiah 33:9)

REFLECTIONS

Questions:
1. Which do you find more challenging: praising God in adverse circumstances, or remembering to exalt God when things are going well?
2. What are some things you might do to cultivate a more consistent attitude of praise? Consider maintaining a daily prayer time, worshiping through music, memorizing and speaking positive Scriptures about who God is and what he can do in your life, and journaling to record the movements of God that you see on a daily basis.

Practical Applications and *Additional Resources:*
If you are experiencing challenges maintaining an attitude of praise, and even struggle with depression and despair, I highly recommend a couple audio seminars by Cindy entitled *Defeating Depression: Cooperating with God to Experience Victory Over Negative Emotions,* and *Muddling Through Motherhood: Experiencing Joy in the Midst of Occasional Chaos.* These resources are available at www.valuesdrivenfamily.com.

For Additional Study:
We see countless illustrations in Scripture of those who chose to praise God when they saw him move—in big ways or in small ways. Just a handful of examples include: the healed cripple (Acts 3:8); Mary, the mother of Jesus (Luke 1:46); Zechariah, upon the dedication of his son (Luke 1:68); the healed lepers (Luke 17:15-16); and the believers after the resurrection (Luke 24:50-53). Let these examples, and others, encourage you to look for God in your life and praise him when you see him in action.

PART FOUR: Parenting on Purpose

> "If anyone sets his heart on being an overseer, he desires a noble task. Now the overseer must be above reproach.... He must manage his own family well and see that his children obey him with proper respect." 1 Timothy 3:1, 2a, 4)

All of us as parents engage in some type of work—in a typical job, working from home in a home-based business, or as a homemaker. For those of us who work away from home, there can be a real disconnect between what we do for eight or ten hours a day, and what our families are doing at home during that same time frame. Due to the lack of overlap between work and family, it can be difficult to piece these two distinct entities together and create a seamless fabric. As such, working from home or being employed in a home-based business can be a very rewarding option for many; in fact, I (Marc) have experienced the benefits of a more flexible work environment that allows me to work from home regularly. Yet even when I worked in a more formal corporate environment I was equally fortunate to have had a unique work experience that helped me to in some way merge the two usually divergent elements of work and family.

As a project manager in both the environmental consulting and electronic document management industries, I have practiced applying management and problem-solving principles to analyzing situations, identifying problems, developing solutions, and implementing those solutions. I have also trained corporate individuals to apply these principles in developing technological solutions and in preparing for project management certification.

How, you may wonder, does this experience relate at all to family? Early on in my career, God really opened my eyes to the great parallels that could, and even should, exist between the business world and the world of the family. While I gained experience in corporate project management, I was taking these principles and practices home—at times with unexpected results. Instead of haphazardly applying this theory or that system, we began parenting "on purpose": with intention and direction.

I've found that all of the solutions and management principles defined and used by successful corporations can be applied to the family unit. In fact, a household is a lot like a business; it encompasses a series of processes with inputs and outputs and involves various players with specific short and long-term goals. The household also has leadership, property, transportation, communication, utilities, and workers, with similar time and cash flow constraints as a business.

A subset of these business principles is the concept of project management, which also has a direct application within the family. The parenting phase of family can certainly be defined as a "project": it has a specific objective, is unique, and has a defined start and end date. As Christian parents, an objective we can all agree on is that we want to raise children who serve the Lord *and* experience peace, joy, and success along the journey. In line with our definition, it is inarguable that all families are unique, and as far as having delineated parameters, parenting clearly starts when the children are born and ceases when they are sent away on their own. Therefore, we can agree that parenting is a *project*.

Businesses are designed to be efficient and productive. Much research and effort has been put into defining management principles because they are vital to the success of companies. Yet, the average household does not operate according to planning principles; on the contrary, we more often drudge along, struggling to keep up with the demands of life. Instead, we should consider taking advantage of these concepts to derive a plan that will meet the challenges facing the average household. These applications can be of great help in achieving our parenting goals in this great journey.

Implementing some of these practical principles within the family helps us optimize our time, strengthen our areas of weakness, and work toward well-defined goals. This is certainly to our benefit—after all, we've all heard the joke, "children don't come with owner's manuals," and it's amusing because it's true! Young couples are thrust into the parenting "project," often ill-equipped for the journey. Regardless of our background, nothing truly prepares us for the life change that comes with parenting.

As we go through parenthood, we may model what our parents did, or may simply pass the time in "survival mode," struggling to get through each day. If you were blessed with exemplary Christian parents who had it all together, great! You are part of a privileged minority. If you are not, some "family process reengineering" is probably in order. What showed us our need in this area was our lack of peace, joy, and success—all the things that we felt God's Word promised us as faithful parents continually eluded us. We, like most parents, knew there was more. That is why we embarked on the journey of family re-definition, growth, and change—seeking to align what we did with what was pleasing to God to maximize our life experience and to ensure that we accomplished God's goals for our family.

In this section of the book we will discuss many of the reigning theories that were developed for business, yet can be applied to the family. It is our hope that you will benefit from the wisdom of the many whose learning and experience have contributed to this body of knowledge. We'll be using some of the terms that have been formalized by businesses, so we'd like to offer a word of caution before we begin: don't get too hung up on the definitions or spend too much time in trying to conceptualize it all—just use the information as a springboard to a more direct application for your household. As you read, we hope that you will apply these principles in your home, in accordance with the Scriptures and with God's desire for us to "make the most of every opportunity" (Ephesians 5:16).

Chapter 22: Managing the Family Project: *An Introduction*

Projects have five processes: initiation, planning, execution, closure, and control. The first four processes are sequential phases and the controlling process occurs during the entire project, with a greater emphasis during execution.

In the family, *initiation* includes both starting a family and making a commitment to childrearing; after all, procreation is *not* synonymous with parenting. In the *planning* phase, we would establish goals and formulate a detailed plan to get there. This is where many of us fall down. Once we make the commitment to be the best parents we can, we often neglect to be proactive and develop a plan. However, once we have one, it must be implemented—this is described as *execution*. During the *controlling* process we take steps to ensure we are tracking on plan. The *closure* phase is "the end," which for us as parents means transitioning our children to autonomy and providing guidance and support on an as-needed basis. Though in the true project management sense all of the phases are discrete, for the sake of simplicity, we will combine some aspects of execution and control in our discussion on planning.

Because the *initiation* stage of family is straight forward, we will describe it here simply by way of introduction to the more relevant material. Subsequent chapters will provide a detailed analysis of the successive phases, where there will be much more practical application of the project management principles within the family unit.

In the business world, project initiation begins with the identification of a need or desire, and the project is authorized by leadership. In the family, it's a tad simpler: Mom and Dad get together and at some point—hopefully by choice—nine months later, the "project" is initiated. An initiation document for the family, if it were thought out, might read something like this: *We want to be good parents, which means pleasing God. As such, our desire is that our children serve God upon emancipation, influencing this world for Christ in future generations. As we raise our children, we want to maintain peace and joy in our home and remain continuously effective in fulfilling God's corporate and unique purposes. We will rely on the guidance of God's Word and look to additional biblical resources to help us in this endeavor.*

In parenting, initiation certainly encompasses more than just deciding to have children; it also means accepting the associated responsibilities. For Christian parents, this may simply mean making a commitment to the disciplines of biblical parenting. Once the course of action is fixed and the various roles and responsibilities are outlined, the project transitions into the next phase, which is *planning*. This is a more detailed phase with a great deal of application within the family; it will be the focus of the next several chapters.

REFLECTIONS

Questions:
1. Honestly assess the current state of your family management. Would you say that you model what your parents did, react to circumstances or are driven by emotions, have a hit-or-miss mentality about trying new or different things, or have a proactive plan for achieving your personal and God-given duties to achieve loftier goals?

For Additional Study:
Study some examples of the supervision (or *government*) of God's people and the planning and implementation of God-ordained projects to see how management principles are put into practice in a biblical context (for example, 1 Kings 4:1-28, 2 Chronicles 31). Also explore verses related to the management of the home and family (for example, 1 Timothy 3:4, 1 Timothy 5:14).

Part Four: Parenting on Purpose

Chapter 23: Planning in Parenthood: *Defining the Scope*

Once we start a family, we should be proactive in planning how we will be faithful to our duties as parents in raising our children to serve the Lord. A vision and a goal are relatively easy to establish, but planning is where the rubber meets the road. It is in the planning phase that all of the variables are to be considered. We will see that the dynamics associated with planning and executing a project are similar to those for planning family success: developing a scope, team building, managing risk, budgets, schedules, defining roles and responsibilities, and staying on target to meet the goals.

This may seem overwhelming—and if you look at it all at once, it is! The key to developing a workable project plan is *decomposition*, or breaking the requirements down to simple, manageable sub-components, one aspect at a time. You can see how we have *decomposed* the discreet components of parenting: training, encouragement, and discipline, and by considering biblical living as a series of core values rather than as the sum of a whole book. Likewise, in this next section, we will look at some of the more practical aspects of planning that are associated with everyday parenting, such as budgets and schedules and the like. If you agree with the premises thus far presented and use the information that follows, your own planning phase of parenting will be relatively simple—you will focus more on the execution and control.

The planning phase typically begins with defining the *scope*: the height, width, and breadth of the project. For us, this would be a bit of a challenge, since the scope of parenting encompasses all of family life; that is, all aspects of the lives of every single family member prior to emancipation. However, we can start with a more general exercise and see what the Scriptures say about how we should direct our thoughts and efforts. This will help us set the stage for more concrete planning by giving us the proper perspective on life and this family adventure.

If we are to remain focused on those things that are important to God, we should keep our minds free from unnecessary distractions. The Bible recommends that we do not concern ourselves with matters out of our control, but rather trust in God and seek his peace. John 44:1 says, "Do not let your hearts be troubled. Trust in God; trust also in me" (see also Philippians 4:6-7).

Concerning ourselves with matters we can't change is foolish. Certainly, we should always be aware of potential challenges or of impending decisions; however, our thoughts should linger on these only insomuch as we can influence them. Our influence may be simply to reach out to the Lord in prayer or to make our circumstances known to someone who might be able to help. Either way, we are not called to *worry* about these matters (meditating on them in an unhealthy way); we must trust in the One who can deliver us. It certainly takes wisdom to recognize what it is *we* should do versus what we should let *God* do! Do what you can, and don't be anxious about things that are out of your control.

In the same way, our thoughts should be most focused on the things of *today* rather than consumed with past events (which cannot be changed) or future events (which are uncertain). Matthew 6:25-34 can help us keep this perspective; it reminds us, "'do not worry about tomorrow, for tomorrow will worry about itself. Each day has enough trouble of its own'" (Matthew 6:34). These verses teach us that we are to *concern ourselves only with today's struggles.* As parents, we know the minute-by-minute challenges of whining toddlers, traffic jams, a phone ringing at the "wrong" time, etc. These struggles are real and consume a lot of our energy, and God does not fail to recognize this. We are not called into freedom from sin to be in bondage to our worries.

This does not mean that we should not *consider* tomorrow. Keep in mind, however, that there is a great distinction between *planning* and *worrying*. To keep our minds clear, we should focus on planning for matters that are within our control; we should simply pray for matters that are out of our control. The Bible says, "The plans of the diligent lead to profit" (Proverbs 21:5a), so we do not ignore the future. However, our thoughts and plans must be directed on those things that we can directly influence, particularly through immediate action.

With this foundational biblical perspective on both daily and future events, let's broaden our scope a bit and flesh out our definitions for the purposes of more proactive planning.

In the project planning arena, a *scope document* will discuss the major deliverables, or end-products, and provide success and completion criteria, time and cost estimates, assumptions, and constraints. Again, don't let the terms overwhelm you—not all of these have a one-to-one application to the family; however, there is a great deal of overlap that will be beneficial to explore.

We have defined two major *deliverables* for family: *children serving God* when they leave home, and *peace and joy in the home during the journey.* A *success criterion* is 100% of children serving God when they are on their own. This may be evaluated based on church attendance, ministry involvement, Bible reading, prayer, regular giving, and, in particular, exhibiting the fruit of the Spirit (Galatians 5:22) and the character of Christ. We track toward this goal by consistently teaching and training in biblical values and precepts and by encouraging and disciplining our children according to God's Word, as outlined previously in Part Two.

One way to assess the level of peace and joy in the home is by evaluating the children's encouragement chart performance; our home atmosphere remains fairly stable when we can encourage the children in achieving the "10 out of 12" goal that we have adopted. Typically, however, we find that peace and joy increase as the children (and parents) strive for a higher standard. Of course, our feelings and emotions are another measure of success.

The *completion criteria* would be defined as children leaving home when they are adults. This would not include going off to college, but rather moving on as self-sufficient adults, no longer under parental authority.

The *assumptions* we make in this values-driven family project are many. We assume that God is real and his Word is true. We assume that abiding by his precepts will result in the blessings promised in the Bible. We believe that children are a blessing, not a burden. We believe that if we do our part, God will do his part. These assumptions lay the groundwork for persevering through this journey.

Defining the scope of parenting serves mainly to provide us with a perspective that will set the stage for more concrete phases of planning. Two of the more practical aspects of family living that require planning include schedules and budgets, which we will explore in more detail in the next chapters.

REFLECTIONS

Questions:
1. If we have a more reactionary style of parenting or focus more on the day-to-day than the long-term (by worrying rather than planning), we may easily overlook the depth and breadth of the scope of biblical parenting and fail to be proactive where needed. If you view parenting more as a project with definitions such as we have outlined in this chapter, how does this affect your perspective on family living?

Practical Applications and *Additional Resources:*
The emotion of worry can keep us from properly planning; it can also keep us from experiencing everyday peace and joy. We've suggested many resources throughout this book—why not look to the Bible and allow God's Word to bring you peace? The Psalms are especially comforting when we are contemplating an uncertain future, finding it hard to wait, or facing a situation that's beyond our control.

For Additional Study:
Think about some of the *assumptions* that may govern your family project—we have already named a few, including trust in God's Word and

his promises, and the belief that as we do our part, God will do his. We can all struggle with our faith in these areas at different points along our long family journey. It may help to do a word study about faith, or about God's faithfulness to us. Consider Scriptures such as Psalm 33:4, Psalm 138:1-3, and Romans 3:3-4.

Chapter 24: The Nuts-and-Bolts of Planning: *Schedules*

It's easy to let time get away from us, whether it's inconvenient drop-in visits from well-meaning friends or relatives, a TV show that distracts us...and then turns into two or three, surfing that endless Web, or those incessant phone calls! There were times when I (Cindy) would look at how few items were checked off of my daily to-do list and wonder, *what happened*? That was a common scenario for me *before* I discovered household scheduling. I wasn't even aware of the concept before our second child or so, and didn't really think we needed one until our third; but once we experienced the productivity and balance that a good schedule promotes, I wondered why we hadn't begun sooner! Though we have now worked our way from a schedule into an "ordered routine," starting with (and sticking to) a schedule for several years was a valuable experience with many benefits for our family.

A schedule is simply a budget-tool for the stewardship of our time, since both time and money are valuable commodities. Just as a business will leverage both budgets and schedules for maximum effectiveness, so can a household benefit from a wise plan for time management.

In the project management world, the schedule is based on a *work breakdown structure* (WBS). The WBS outlines the activities that are required to reach the objectives and breaks them down into tasks and discrete work packages. These *work packages* are assigned to workers and put on a timeline, or sequenced. In comparative terms, activities are broader in scope, while tasks are narrower and work packages are the most specific.

The Family Breakdown

For the values-driven family, we have already identified the objectives in our sample scope; now we simply need to break down the work into activities, tasks, and work packages. We have found that our family "project" activities fall into four basic categories: *work, family, spiritual (or ministry),* and *rest*. These elements, when properly managed, help us maintain health and balance in the home. Although God has Kingdom purposes, we cannot neglect the practical matters of everyday family living as we pursue these grander goals. In fact, wisely balancing these four different quadrants of life is what ultimately helps us to achieve God's goals.

God ordained *work* for man from the very beginning (Genesis 2:15, 3:23) and we are admonished to "work with our hands" so that our needs will be met and we will earn the respect of others (see 1 Thessalonians 4:11-12). The importance of *family* is equally clear throughout the Scriptures, whether in reference to the marital relationship (Ephesians 5:33) or to the parent/child relationship (for example, Titus 2:4, Proverbs 3:12). We are also called to attend to our *spiritual* needs, which means putting our God-given gifts and abilities to work for his glory (Romans 12:6-8).

Yet there is a necessity and a time for *rest*, which will refresh us in the Lord for greater service (Exodus 34:21, Mark 6:31). The activity we label as *rest* breaks down into a number of different tasks, including exercise and nutrition. This is because the disciplines of healthy eating and regular exercise energize and refresh us to help us best fulfill our family roles and God-given purposes. Remember, the Bible does tell us to honor God with our bodies (see 1 Corinthians 6:20).

Rest also encompasses sleep and leisure, which, in proper proportion, are necessary and beneficial. Mom occasionally needs a break from the children as much as Dad needs a break from work. Mom and Dad need quality time together as well as alone time with God. Families need times away from the home and from household routines now and then as well. These breaks help us maintain physical, emotional, and spiritual wholeness. Incorporating these needs into the family routine will ensure that the family relationships will remain strong and the family duties will get accomplished without burnout or excessive frustration. One way to maintain a proper balance of rest along with our other activities is to remember that God worked for six days and only rested for one!

Bringing the functional matters of family into balance with God's Kingdom purposes is a challenge—but as we seek God and determine to live by his values and precepts, the pieces of the puzzle fall more easily into place, particularly with the help of a good schedule. Living balanced lives brings us peace and assures us that we will be addressing all of the vital areas in their proper proportion.

Building a Schedule: First Steps and General Considerations

For ease of reference, we'll categorize the general activities of everyday life according to this quadrant structure, summarized in the following table.

Work	*Family*	*Spiritual*	*Rest*
Work for Income	Child Training	Prayer	Sleep
Home Management	Encouragement	Devotions	Exercise
	Relationships	Fellowship	Nutrition
	Discipline	Discipleship	Leisure
	Education	Service	
	Socialization	Evangelism	
	General Childcare		

With this groundwork laid, next you would determine the more specific tasks and work packages associated with each activity and decide who will be responsible for each one (husband, wife—or both—or, the children). By way of example, let's further break down the activity of *Home Management* by listing the individual tasks, with work packages in parentheses: Housekeeping (Individual Cleaning Tasks, Laundry); Food Preparation (Grocery Shopping, Menu Planning, Set-up and Clean-up, Cooking); Shopping (Clothing, Household supplies, Gifts); Accounting and Bookkeeping (Budget Creation and Tracking, Checkbook Balance, Bill Payment); Property Maintenance (Auto Repair and Maintenance, Yard Maintenance, Home Repair or Remodeling).

Some activities in the table may be considered discrete tasks in and of themselves (such as *Exercise*), while you will want to individualize others as your personal circumstances dictate. One way to get a better idea of your personal responsibilities is to keep a time log for a couple of weeks, before trying to formalize a schedule. List your activities every 15 or 30 minutes to see what you typically accomplish during each day. This is also a great way to identify and guard against time drains that can really affect the success of your time management plan. You will also want to consider both your long- and short-term goals in determining your short-range schedules.

Once you have considered the basic activities that have already been enumerated in the table or identified through your time log, you will break down larger activities into smaller tasks as needed, such as we have done by example with Home Management. Finally, consider the more specific work packages. Then, broadly define "who" will usually be assigned to each one of these tasks or work packages.

Certainly, your work breakdown and the assignment of tasks will be unique and will depend on many things, such as whether or not both Mom and Dad work for income. If this is the case, there will most likely be a greater sharing of other responsibilities. The idea is to identify your usual activities and be aware of who will do what on a routine basis. Clearly establishing the roles and responsibilities of family members is a vital prerequisite to setting up schedules for accomplishing all of the family objectives and for minimizing conflict.

Once the tasks are assigned (and each worker is aware of his or her responsibilities), the various components can then be put into a schedule. Managing our schedules to give all four of life's core quadrants their due is certainly a challenge. It seems that there is always something to do and not enough time to get to everything; however, there is exactly enough time to do every single thing that God wants us to get done. Much of the time, though, our busyness is self-induced. We get our children involved in every activity, we agree to participate in every church program, we commit to going to every family picnic and birthday party, we take a job with a 55-minute commute because it pays five thousand per year more, and we acquire many possessions that all demand care and maintenance. These are burdens that we put on ourselves.

If you have trimmed your list of duties down as far as it can go and you still can't get it all done, you may have to re-evaluate your standards as well as your various activities. Life has many seasons and during some periods of life, concessions have to be made. When you have a newborn, during certain stages of pregnancy, if you are taking a class in addition to your work, during an intensive church event, or following a death in the family—these are all seasons in which the standards may need to be compromised a little. Or better yet, ask for help.

Also look carefully at your activities and see where you can accommodate some multi-tasking. This is especially important if you home school. If we are running errands, the children may bring some reading along in the car, or some drill and practice worksheets on a clipboard that can be worked on during the commute. We've also used a children's foreign language tape series and workbook, which occasionally we have played on the car's cassette player to make good use of the time. We use grocery shopping and cooking as opportunities to apply math concepts, like unit cost, dollars off for sales, change back from purchases, and basic addition, subtraction, fractions, and multiplication. There are many teachable opportunities that we can leverage in daily life.

We've also looked for ways to nurture our marriage by multi-tasking—one (perhaps unusual) thing we did at our prior house was to install an oversized whirlpool tub in our master bathroom, and it had a shower head on both sides. Because we have to allot time for a daily shower anyway, we decided to multi-task and shower together, which is a great way to add an extra 15 minutes of uninterrupted conversation into our schedule. With some creativity, multi-tasking can be a great benefit to your schedule as you strive to do all the things that God wants you to do.

Implementing a schedule and assigning tasks also demands that we have reasonable expectations. As parents, we must be realistic about what a child can accomplish in a given time frame. Likewise, we may want to be done with grocery shopping in a one-hour window, but given travel time and the likelihood of waiting in line, we are wise to adjust our expectations.

Husbands and wives should also consider each others' time burdens and capacity to be successful with the tasks at hand.

When scheduling, work around your fixed daily events (such as personal hygiene, meal times, naps, school times, and so on). Aim for consistency so that everyone has a general idea of what to expect and can function productively even if the written "schedule" is not available.

Scheduling Considerations

You may want to refrain from scheduling your weekends, since these are more likely to be subject to whims of family members and changing calendars of events. One thing that we have never compromised, however, is our Saturday "Mommy/Daddy date night." This is a priority for us because it helps us maintain a healthy marital relationship. We don't go out on a formal date very often, but at the very least, we try to eat our dinner in the living room while the children eat in the dining room. Although there are bound to be interruptions, it's an opportunity for a little bit of adult conversation, and it models for our children the importance of marriage partners making time for each other in the busyness of life. On these nights, we put the children to bed at 7:00 (either for early sleep or quiet reading/talking in bed), and we may watch a movie, play cards, talk, or just relax together—"whatever!" This is just one example of how family objectives can be met through flexible scheduling.

We also never scheduled our after-dinner hours, but we do maintain a set routine of things that get done on particular days of the week, whether work projects, family fun nights, core value lessons, or Bible study.

When it comes to children's schedules, keep in mind that young children can only manage about 30 minutes of a single activity. Also, they will need a plan that alternates high-energy and quiet activities.

And don't be too quick to overlook the benefits of infant schedules as well. Although we don't formalize a schedule of specific times for infant feedings, sleeping, etc., we have seen the incredible value of establishing a general *routine* for babies, right from the moment of birth. One day the baby may nurse every 3 hours, the next day every 2-1/2; it's important to allow that flexibility to meet the baby's needs, but also important to aim for consistency and set limits as necessary (for example, distinguishing between a baby's need for nutrition and desire to use her mother as a pacifier!). Although you may not set specific times for these infant activities, a baby can and should be trained, as much as possible, to accommodate the rhythms of the household in regard to wake/sleep and social times, in particular. This helps keep the entire family functioning more smoothly when a new baby is welcomed into the fold.

We try to parse our schedule (and even our now-daily routines) into 30-minute components. If you have young children to attend to, it is not realistic for you (or them!) to focus on a task for longer than this. You may just have to split more involved tasks in two. For example, sweep the floors on day 1 and mop them on day 2; or, sweep in the morning and mop in the afternoon. This will reduce frustration on your part and avoid you neglecting the children or sitting them in front of the television to keep them out of your way.

Planning and scheduling is also much more effective when external drivers are minimized. Doctor's appointments, family gatherings, and church events are certain to be a staple part of any household. However, involving every child in multiple extracurricular activities (and each one, something different!) is most certain to create imbalance. Be practical and proactive in establishing realistic plans for your family.

Likewise, consider those time sinks that take away from things we *should* be doing: for example, television, phone, and Internet. Trade wasted time for productive time. Entertainment has its place in maintaining emotional health, and you may choose some television programming to relax your mind or offer some learning opportunities; however, this should be proactive and scheduled to ensure that more important things are not being neglected.

Likely, those who work full time for income will not have as formal a schedule such as will benefit the homemaker and children, since a wage-earner's daily schedule is set by his or her employer. This person will just want to develop a general routine for evening and weekend hours that allows for the accomplishment of all his or her duties.

Schedule Set-up

For the homemaker and the children: to actually establish a schedule, you will want to "begin with the end in mind" and prioritize all of your normal tasks and work packages. Choose a scheduling format, such as noting occasional events on a monthly calendar and integrating those activities into your daily schedule as necessary. Experiment with different methods of inputting and tracking these daily events; for example, the calendar feature of your computer's email program (or another planning software), an editable table in Microsoft Word, the traditional pen-and-paper method, or perhaps using a commercially available planner.

Using the method of your choice, plan each week in advance according to whatever time frame works best for you. Personally, I (Cindy) scheduled my days from 6:30 AM when the children woke up until 6:00 PM, which is usually dinner time.

As you schedule activities, keep your natural rhythms in mind. If you are a morning person, you may want to concentrate your more energy-intensive activities (such as housekeeping) in the morning hours, while reserving sit-down action items like bill payment or correspondence for afternoons or evenings.

As a starting point for your planning, you will input recurring events in order of priority (for example, time for personal hygiene, family Bible reading and prayer, work, sports practice and game schedules, church events such as youth group, etc.). Remember, each member of the family (ideally) will have his or her own schedule; however, you can list multiple schedules on the same sheet for ease of use by using a format that incorporates a number of columns for each time period.

Block out fixed items, then fill in the vital items that have some flexibility. We start with sleep schedules for the children, working daily activities around nap schedules and meal times. Then fill in other activities, ensuring that all the family objectives are met.

For ease of use, it is best to have a general schedule for each day that will remain basically the same. However, if you have days of the week that vary greatly in their routines, you may want to have a schedule for each of the days that are similar, and a different schedule for the alternate day(s). I found this helpful for a while; we were involved in a home school co-op two days per week, which forced enough changes to our morning and pre-nap routines that it was easier to have two entirely different schedules.

Because I used to try to maintain a fairly set schedule, one issue that arose was the need for flexibility in accommodating intermittent or alternating work packages. To solve this problem, I put some generic time slots into my schedule in addition to the more specific everyday events.

For example, I have a routine for housekeeping in which I wash the kitchen floor one week and the bathroom floors the next week; one week I dust the bedrooms and alternate weeks I dust the living and dining rooms. Instead of inputting these as specific tasks on my weekly planner, I simply schedule 30 minutes in the morning and 30 minutes in the afternoon for "housekeeping," and I have a separate listing of these alternating tasks. After a while, it has become such an ingrained routine that I no longer need my list—but it's there for reference. Likewise, once a week I may catch up on correspondence, another day I will I balance the checkbook or pay bills, and at other times I may need to do lesson planning or grading for home school. These tasks all get accomplished as needed during a block of time that I simply schedule as "record keeping" time.

Because of this variability, I have found that a daily to-do list is a necessary complement to my weekly schedule. And, if you're like me, you will feel a great sense of accomplishment as you cross those action items off your list throughout the day—it can be a great motivator!

Although a schedule is a good way to bring order to our day and ensure that we are meeting all of the demands of life, flexibility is necessary for the successful management of a family. Sickness, or any one of countless other factors, can certainly impact the plan. We must also be sure we allow room for *God* to change our well-laid plans if he has something else in mind. Always remember that God values people and his purposes more than man-made rules, even the most well-thought-out schedules. Yet, at the same time,

145

do guard against allowing too many interruptions in your schedule, even if it is via phone or email. It's important to strike a balance for maximum effectiveness in home management.

Flexibility should also not become synonymous with *laziness*. Discipline is necessary in implementing a schedule; deviations from the plan should be exceptions, not the rule. In the area of time management, consistency rules the day. It is amazing how much both we and our children appreciate the schedules. They look at their charts and go to their jobs without even asking sometimes. They know what the evening plan is just based on the day of the week. Their routine is set and it is known. It is accepted and everyone knows what to expect. We find that there is less misbehavior and a more general calm in the home when things progress with regularity and stability. Schedules are definitely a beneficial tool for the entire family.

A Reasonable Alternative: Building a Solid Routine

*S*cheduling is a loaded word, and often inspires dread in the mom who just hasn't gotten the hang of it yet. We've just gone into great detail about how I (Cindy) used to do it. I used to love it. But in a way, I used to hate it, too. Why? Because for as many days as a schedule helped me to feel productive, there were days that the productivity was at the expense of relationship-building, discipleship opportunities with the children, and what have you—things, frankly, that were more important than what was on my schedule. My schedule too often ruled the day! Really, it was no fault of the schedule, but rather a matter of how I viewed and used this beneficial tool.

If you read my more recent book, *The Growing Homeschool*, you will see a paradigm shift in the focus, from *schedule* to *routine*. Now, instead of scheduling every day and every task to the half-hour and feeling guilty when it's not done (or allowing those tasks to drive us and feeling guilty about missed opportunities), we have developed a solid routine for our days that is based on our well-defined priorities.

However, don't throw the baby out with the bath water upon hearing about this philosophic change. A rather lengthy period of using a schedule was necessary for us, and highly beneficial in many ways. Scheduling helped us grow in necessary self-discipline. It helped us to examine our daily tasks and see where our time was going. It helped us to be better stewards of our time. I wouldn't "not" recommend it as a tool for *making the most of every opportunity*.

On the other hand, we have found that having routine-based day allows us to be more responsive to the Holy Spirit's leading and enables us to better fulfill *God's* plans for our day. At the same time, there is enough structure to promote necessary self-discipline and ensure that there is a time for everything. It seems an ideal balance.

The Foundations of a Good Routine

So with practice in scheduling, how do you shift into a solid routine that will ensure that all of your vital priorities are being met? Well, the first thing you need to do is decide what those priorities are, and try to set them in order of importance. Husband and wife need to talk together about what is most important to each of them, and why, since there will not always be instant agreement. However, this is a vital conversation, and much stress and frustration can be avoided when both partners are on the same page.

How is this helpful? Well, oftentimes I "think" that the house is a mess and so home management becomes *priority one*. I get to bustling around the house and pretty soon I'm telling the kids, "Sure, I'll be there in a minute. Just as soon as I'm done with [insert task]." But, I think back on my husband's priorities. He wants the house to be "neat" so that we are prepared to practice hospitality and be welcoming to potential guests in an instant. However, he prefers to invest the maximum amount of time in relationship-building, life skills, and discipleship opportunities. When I find myself cleaning "too much," I know that I'm not doing my best to meet *my husband's* expectations—and frankly, I trust in his wisdom to lead our home and know that his choices are probably better than mine (even if my perfectionist instincts disagree). So I switch gears and drop what I'm doing, then get back on track with the higher priorities.

Your husband's duties may be different from yours and will most likely include providing for the family through work. You may or may not need to be concerned with that. I'm talking here about the priorities that will guide *your* day as you manage your home and possibly homeschool. What does your husband think you should focus on? What are your preferences as to how time will be spent? Some couples will agree that academics are important and should be addressed as a priority in homeschooling; other families focus on discipleship as the heart of their homeschool. You don't have to agree with "everyone else," but you and your husband must be in agreement as to how things will work in *your* home.

Some things to consider in setting your priorities and putting them in order are:

- Work for income, if it is necessary for you
- Discipleship of your children (teaching and modeling God's Word, and bringing the Scriptures alive through everyday "teachable moments")
- Ministry opportunities in your community
- Building family relationships
- Homeschooling (and your focus: academic, life-skills oriented, or discipleship-based, as well as the amount of paperwork/planning you need to do to meet state requirements or fulfill your personal obligations)

- Home management (housekeeping, grocery shopping, bill payment, and all the things that go along with it)

For us, we view discipleship and family relationships as priority one; ministry opportunities are usually second in line, then homeschooling (however, integrating all-of-the-above is the ideal). My home-based work for income usually ties in last place with home management—and home management is usually the more pressing of the two. However, there are seasons where I'm working on a project and home management takes a back seat. However, I try to coordinate those projects with a school vacation or part-time schedule of schooling if need be, so that I'm not overwhelmed and so that everything can be reasonably accomplished.

What if we are expecting company? Well, home management is likely the more important task of the day, and we might call a "work day" and the children will get excused from some of their homeschooling to help. The next day may be spent on academic "catch up."

From these two examples alone, you can see why a *routine* is preferable to a *schedule*! Each day is different, and some days our priorities have to be re-ordered according to circumstances. However, those priorities are a necessary guide in the midst of the busyness of day-to-day life.

A routine is also preferable because on some days, accomplishing those priorities takes different amounts of time and cannot be neatly segmented into the 30-minute increments of the typical daily schedule. Occasionally it seems like we're capitalizing on one "teachable moment" after another (read: *some days the kids seem to be getting into all kinds of trouble, and bickering about everything, and not doing their jobs!*) However, that's discipleship at its best—and that's a priority! Other days may be light on discipleship, so we will focus on homeschooling or home management and get a lot done to "make up" for any lost time.

Truthfully, I think that the difference between a schedule and a routine is *faith*. Are we seeking God and prayerfully doing our best to do what *He* wants us to do? Are we listening to the quiet voice of the Holy Spirit as He prompts us to change direction? Can we be flexible enough to submit to God's plan, particularly when it is adversity or annoyances that reveal the change in direction? If so, then a routine is an ideal tool and allows us to accomplish all that is in God's will for our day. Conversely, a rigid and unforgiving schedule only causes us to try to "do it all" in our own strength—and *that* can be quite frustrating! But remember, "In his heart a man plans his course, but the Lord determines his steps" (Proverbs 16:9).

Putting Routines into Practice

Now, how about taking a look at some of the more specific routines that we have found helpful to integrate into our days? This may give you a good "starting point" in deciding how to shape *your* day.

As we proactively set routines in place, we find that things run more smoothly and bad attitudes are generally squelched before they rear their ugly heads—regardless of life's circumstances. The daily routines that we have found most helpful are: family devotions, personal Bible reading and prayer, chore times, daily training times, and character training. You will notice that "school time" is not one of the routines. Yes, this needs to be part of your time organization/schedule if you homeschool, but (for us, anyway) it is *not* one of the essential foundations. The essential foundations, you will notice, have more to do with *being* than with *doing*—and these are the things that affect our attitudes and actions the most. By attending to these "first things first," the day-to-day "doings" are a lot easier on everyone.

For us, each day starts with *family devotions*. We get together in the living room and spend a short time reading the Bible and praying together. There's no "magic" to it, and no particular formula—but when we don't get our day started off on the right foot with this routine, it usually isn't long before we realize we've missed it! I love the words of Psalm 5:3: "In the morning, O LORD, you hear my voice; in the morning I lay my requests before you and wait in expectation." As we focus on the Lord in the morning, we certainly go into the day "expecting" God's presence and His answer to prayer. You will find more specific guidance for daily discipleship (including family devotions) in our *Values-Driven Discipleship* manual. Of all the daily routines, this one is the most important.

As well, individual family members try to set aside *personal time with the Lord*. I (Cindy) usually manage to get up a bit earlier than everyone else, and I love the "quiet time!" The children all have Bible and prayer time after breakfast, older children with their Bibles and younger children with storybook versions. The pre-readers often convene on the upstairs couch to "read" Bible stories together and discuss them with me; the older children usually separate to the bedroom or downstairs couch so the little ones don't disturb them. We try not to be legalistic about the children having this time, as we don't want to make Bible reading seem like a punishment or a burden; rather, we began this routine with a gentle daily encouragement: "Why don't we all grab a Bible and read for a few minutes, to see what God has for us today!" We also don't associate any "rules" or assignments with this time. I have told the children that I sometimes use a journal in my quiet time, other times copy down and memorize Bible verses, sometimes study with a concordance, or otherwise just read. Much as my own devotional time varies, so does theirs. I may ask them about their quiet time or what they have read, but there is no pressure to perform. This has made daily times with the Lord a happier habit for everyone to develop.

Another proactive part of our daily routines that keeps things on a consistently even keel is *chore time*. It takes some time to train the children in doing chores, but with patience, good modeling, positive encouragement, and (later) quality-control checks, it is an investment well worth the pay-off.

(We'll talk more about that later.) Daily chore times are a good habit that helps to maintain a general sense of order and peace in the home.

Daily training times are one of my favorite routines; we've talked about this a bit already. Sometimes our daily training times are brief (5 minutes) and sometimes they are as much as a half-hour in length—but they are always beneficial. Any time we see something that needs work (or if we want to proactively address certain areas so as not to get to that point), we engage in a fun and enjoyable "training time" to address these topics. We train in safety issues, like fire escape and what to do if you get lost from Mom or Dad in a public place. We train in manners (how to interrupt adult conversations politely, saying "please" and "thank you" and table manners). Other training topics include: picking up toys, putting away toys, shoes, or toothbrushes in their proper places, and even baby care.

We also try to *capitalize on everyday "teachable moments"* and bring the Scriptures into our everyday experiences. While this is not a "routine," per se, it is arguably one of the most valuable habits that we have developed. Family devotions and personal Bible time are important daily routines, but learning to view everyday actions, reactions, and decisions in the light of God's Word has most powerfully affected our children's heart attitudes, character, and (ultimately) behaviors. One way we *do* try to make *character training* more of a routine is, of course, to use the "Core Value Progress Chart" every evening with our children, to encourage their growth in Christlikeness and discuss ways they can improve in doing things "God's way."

Even if you successfully use a daily schedule and continue to find it helpful, sometimes it is difficult to introduce new "doings"—or perhaps just to have everyone stay on-task with a cheerful attitude! You may encounter bad attitudes in response to daily events or even schedule changes; if that is the case, perhaps you will find it helpful to take a step back to focus on some of these essential foundations. Implementing daily family devotional times, having personal time with the Lord, attending to chores on a daily basis, and training in practical matters all reap great rewards as family members strive to grow in Christ together. Whether you formally schedule or opt for a looser routine, it's important that everyone in the family stay "on the same page" and aim for consistency.

REFLECTIONS

Questions:
1. When it comes to your current home management plan, do your daily activities vary greatly, do you try to maintain a general routine, or have you established a more definitive schedule? If you have not used a schedule, what is keeping you from doing so? If you have, would you benefit from shifting to a routine paradigm?

Practical Applications and ***Additional Resources:***

Need to get more organized? We recommend you take a look at the *Organized Mom's Super Set* by our friend Cindy Rushton at www.cindyrushton.com. It isn't cheap, but is a great value for such a comprehensive package.

For Additional Study:

Consider Luke 12:42-43 (with italics added for emphasis) as a reflection of God's value for time management: "The Lord answered, 'Who then is the faithful and wise manager, whom the master puts in charge of his servants to give them their food allowance *at the proper time*? It will be good for that servant whom the master finds doing so when he returns." Study this and other Scriptures that relate to time stewardship (for example, Proverbs 20:4, Ecclesiastes 3:1).

Part Four: Parenting on Purpose

Chapter 25: The Dreaded "B" Word: *Budget*!

Personally, we've gone through many different financial seasons. As a young married couple, we found that we could be pretty free with our money, since we had two incomes and comparatively few expenditures. As we began to consider the future, however, we had to plan for things like home purchase and all of the expenses associated with raising a family—particularly if Mom was to stay at home with the children, which is something we really desired. Slowly but surely we explored different methods of budgeting and found something that worked for us. Although it was an acquired discipline to remain accountable to a budget, we have found that financial stewardship is an absolute necessity in meeting God's goals for our family and using the resources he has given us in the way that he desires.

Financial allocation and planning are important in business, and the Scriptures concur. The parable of the shrewd manager (Luke 16:1-12) is just one example. We can liken God to the rich man who entrusts his possessions to certain managers. We are the managers who must be wise (and self-controlled) with these resources—and we must be able to account for them. This parable shows us how vital it is to properly manage all of the resources, financial and otherwise, that God entrusts to us.

A budget is a vital *planning* tool with which we can track income and expenses in a systematic way, to provide real-time information as well as control and accountability. It can assure us that we are able to provide for today's needs and helps us plan for tomorrow. Consistent use of a budget keeps us aware of our financial situation and reduces anxiety about how much we have versus how much we have to spend. This is a certainly good thing! When viewed properly, budgets, like schedules, become not a restriction but a tool that brings great freedom.

We should view a budget as our friend, because by remaining faithful to a budget we are able to accomplish all of our goals. However, for a budget to work, all spenders must cooperate and submit to the plan. No over-spending can occur in one area without making equal adjustments in another (in other words, you must rob Peter to pay Paul). This takes a common commitment to fiscal stewardship, accountability to the budget, proper communication, and flexibility on the part of all parties involved.

The Workings of a Successful Budget

The budget *must* balance, with all expenditures in consideration (this would include savings and debt-reduction, if they are goals). If it does not, expenses must be reduced or the income must go up. There are no exceptions.

In order for a budget to be helpful, it should not simply provide post-mortem reviews of how you did the prior month. Rather, it is most helpful to consistently track your current expenditures so that each user knows how much money is remaining (per category, in real-time). Yes, to do this right, receipts must be collected and input in the budget, much like a check registry. This is only effective if both partners save receipts.

From our experience, a good budget will allow for flexibility in spending month by month. Some bills are periodic (quarterly, semi-annual, etc.) or are variable (such as utilities and gas, for example). Some budgets will recommend that you input all of your expenses according to their expected payment schedule; however, with things like fuel oil, you may not know in advance when you will need to fill your tank. For us, we have large grocery bills when we shop at a warehouse club, but the next month we will not need to do any shopping—and these events are not always predictable.

Here's how we've addressed this variability in our own budgeting: we set our goal of spending for the year, with an allotment of money for each category, each month. We've acknowledged, however, that some budget categories must allow for overspending in a given month, while still meeting our annual goal for *overall* spending. For example, we may budget $100 per month for car insurance, saving that money in our account—yet we may decide to pay two semi-annual bills of $600 each. On the month that the bill is paid, we may be over budget within that category (since the allowable spending would be set at $100), but we will either have saved that money in advance (over the prior months) or it will be recouped in the coming months.

A good budget will be dynamic to allow adjustment for change. If the income goes up, or expenses unexpectedly go up, the users must be able to adjust the categories on the fly to remain on plan and accommodate the new reality.

You do not necessarily need a computer and software to do a budget. You *can* just do the math with a hand calculator and set up your budget on paper. For ease of use, however, particularly in tracking your expenses in real-time, you may want to explore some of the budget programs that are commercially available. We have authored our own budget tool, which is a very comprehensive Microsoft Excel workbook; it is a low-cost, high-impact tool, available at www.valuesdrivenfamily.com. The tool implements all the suggestions offered in this section, intuitively and without many unnecessary or extraneous features.

The Budgeting Process

Research your spending for the previous several months (or as much as a year), and tabulate your expenses. Start with the fixed expenses, such as rent, car payment, insurance, church giving, etc. Then calculate an average for regular (but not fixed) expenses, like utilities, gas, and groceries. Finally, estimate irregular expenses—car repairs, vacations, gifts, and the like. Next, determine your spendable income (after taxes).

Calculate the difference. If it is negative, start by reducing discretionary spending. If you are still "in the red," you may have some tough decisions to make. You must either sell the items you are currently financing (such as cars) in lieu of more affordable items that you can purchase outright, or you may have to consider getting a second job, or a higher paying job. If your budget calculations are positive, the remaining amount is what you have available for discretionary spending, savings, or debt reduction. Ideally, you will assign categories for all of your income so that you have a net zero, balanced budget. Treat savings as a bill and literally transfer your money from the checking to savings account. Otherwise, saving will likely not occur.

Look at the spending distribution and see for yourself how it measures up to God's values and how balanced it is with respect to life's quadrants. Is your discretionary spending all for pleasure (rest, personal possessions, or dining out), and gifts (family), or are you supporting God's work beyond the tithe (ministry)? Prayerfully consider any realignment.

Budget Execution and Control

To use the budget, simply track your spending by category in real-time and remain on plan per category, with the exception of irregular expenses and seasonally variable expenses. For these categories, track to remain on plan annually and track the total budget monthly to ensure that you are not spending beyond your income for the *total* budget. Remember, for irregular expenses, if you do not spend on month one, the money should technically remain in your checking account and be available for double spending on month two. Therefore, do not rely on your check register to see how much money you have for any single spending category. Rely on the budget. This way you will have the money when you need it.

If you are tracking over-budget for a particular category, reduce your allowable spending in another discretionary category, real-time. This will keep you on plan for the total monthly and annual budgets. This may mean that in a month when you are paying a variable bill, there will be less personal spending, or you may have to make temporary sacrifices; however, over the long-term, everything is brought into balance. That's the idea.

Frugal Living

Budgeting may be necessary in helping you curb your actual purchase of things, but you may still battle with a desire to acquire. Having a mentality of *frugal living* is another important element of financial stewardship, and one that you should seek if you desire greater self-control in this area or just can't make ends meet.

Most people assume that things are far more expensive than they need to be. If accustomed to living on two incomes, families can quickly acclimate to a certain standard of living, expect certain desires to always be fulfilled, or think they *have* to purchase everything new. However, much of what we consider necessities in life are just conveniences. Sacrificing conveniences for the sake of keeping Mom home or pursuing full-time ministry, advanced education, or other goals is a noble decision.

What does this mean, practically? In the area of groceries (which is usually one of the larger expenses for a household), it may mean relying on staple foods (hamburger, whole chicken, lentils, rice, etc.) rather than pre-packaged or extravagant foods; coupon shopping or warehouse-club shopping; making your own bread, toothpaste or other commonly purchased conveniences—even household cleaners! There is a recipe for just about every household product located somewhere on the Internet.

When it comes to our spending habits and purchases, we may have to purchase second-hand wares, from cars to clothing and everything in between. There are tag sales in season, e-Bay year-round if you have Internet access, consignment shops in most towns, or friends who no longer need things and are looking to give them away. We may also need to consider some sacrifices, like that cell phone, dining out, or even cable television. These luxuries are far less important than the spiritual health and well-being of our children.

It also helps the budget to have a do-it-yourself mentality when it comes to auto maintenance and repair or home repairs. Buy (or check out of your local library) a home do-it-yourself book, or purchase the repair manual for your car. If necessary, ask a friend to help you the first time you attempt something unfamiliar, if you are insecure. Then you will have a money-saving skill for life! Marc has found that it is always cheaper in the long run to try a project himself, with the estimate that about one in 10 projects will require the assistance of a professional—either to finish or potentially re-do his work.

If these suggestions aren't enough to keep your budget balanced, there are the major expenses and decisions: trading down to a smaller home or buying a home in a more affordable region of the country, changing jobs, taking an additional job, having Mom work days and Dad work nights, or choosing a home-based or Internet-based job (part time) for Mom.

Think outside the box! There are so many resources available to do life in a different way. There are national Internet communities that post all kinds of free stuff (www.freecycle.org is just one example—you can post a request and get instant responses!). Many sites (like www.miserlymoms.com) offer great tips for more frugal living. Your church can also be a great resource if your income doesn't quite meet your expenditures.

Also consider multi-purpose uses to streamline your expenses *and* make the best use of your resources. Our prior home was of moderate size and we were accommodating a growing number of people—as well as home schooling, which makes even a big house seem small at times. For a while, our basement room doubled as both a recreation room and a school room; we had a folding table that stored chairs underneath and this was set up for schooling. After school, it was folded up and stored in a discreet corner, and we had some comfy, folding "dish chairs" that we hung on the wall, which could be taken out to read books, relax, or watch a movie. This kept the room free from too much clutter and made for a much wiser use of space.

Likewise, when we needed to accommodate multiple children in one small bedroom, we took the double doors off of the closet and found that the little open alcove perfectly fit a baby crib, leaving the main room open for a bed (and later, bunk beds).

To cut down on the clutter and the disorder that can accompany free play time, we have used our hall closet as a combination "toy library" (on the bottom shelves) and linen closet (on the upper shelves). Many of the children's toys are stacked on these lower shelves in clear, closed containers, and the children can check out one at a time during their play time. We encourage them to cooperatively share toys so that there is minimal mess, and the toys maintain their interest because they aren't always available. Not to mention, when we have company it doesn't appear that the children have overtaken our home!

These are some very simple suggestions that may enable you to maximize your effectiveness as parents by taking better control of your finances and better managing the resources that you *do* have. But remember: God is ultimately concerned with the condition of our hearts. If we are willing to live frugally in order to better fulfill God's purposes for our families, we will be blessed. Hebrews 13:5 tells us, "Keep your lives free from the love of money and be content with what you have, because God has said, 'Never will I leave you; never will I forsake you.'" God will show us the areas in which we can make any financial sacrifices that are necessary. Therefore, make God your focus, not your finances, and not the things that you feel you are giving up. If you step out in faithfulness and do what is required for better fiscal stewardship, God will bring the increase and will likely restore your standard of living.

Of course, benefiting from the conveniences in life is *not* wrong. If you have the money, take advantage of these great things! However, we have not, in good conscience, been able to choose these luxuries if it has been at the expense of our children's spiritual health or the financial well-being of our household. In all things, our personal goal has been to make sure our children are benefiting from living in the healthiest environment possible and we are meeting all of our obligations as parents and God's servants.

Ultimately, it is far more important to pursue God's purposes and plans for our lives than it is for us to be financially well-off. We are to hope in the Lord, not put out trust in our worldly wealth (see 1 Timothy 6:17-19). It is wise to manage our finances as best we are able, but this should be done with the goal of honoring God, not just keeping up with the Joneses and meeting a certain social standard. Using a budget will help us arrive at God's financial, practical, and spiritual goals for our family.

REFLECTIONS

Questions:
1. Consider your experience (or lack thereof) with budgeting. If you have not used a budget faithfully, why? We have found that the greatest precursor to making the outward commitment is an inner heart change that only God can accomplish. You may want to commit some thought and prayer to defining any areas where the Lord may want to prompt change.

Practical Applications and *Additional Resources:*
We have authored an incredibly easy-to-use and implement budgeting system that revolves around a handy, yet very powerful, Microsoft Excel-based tool. You may purchase a copy of this tool as part of the home management bundle at www.valuesdrivenfamily.com.

For Additional Study:
Many Scriptures emphasize the importance of financial management, debt freedom, and proper attitude about possessions; study verses such as Proverbs 22:7, Proverbs 10:22, Luke 12:15-21, and Matthew 6:19-34.

Chapter 26: Risk Management

I (Cindy) remember well how scary it was for me, being not yet a Christian, when Marc came home from work one day and put his Bible on the table, saying, "If this is true, then we are going to live by it." I knew things were going to change, and I knew it probably would get uncomfortable from time to time. It wasn't long afterward, though, that I put my trust in Jesus and came into agreement with Marc about how important it was that we live according to God's Word.

As much as this was certainly a defining moment in our Christian life, I also will never forget our son Isaiah's first Halloween, when I had to explain to my mother that we were choosing not to have our children dress up and celebrate the day. Making those difficult decisions is one thing; sticking with them in the face of opposition can be even more challenging. What has made it somewhat easier for us, over time, is the knowledge that we've made the best decisions possible based on the information at hand. We've looked at the benefits of things and counted the cost—and if the cost was too great, we've been able to stand firmly by our convictions.

In project management, this cost/benefit analysis and the planning associated with it are called *risk management*. As parents (or should I say, project managers), we are similarly responsible for managing risk, which is simply to consider all of the potential pitfalls associated with our life's decisions and plan accordingly. The risks inherent in the parenting project are numerous. However, ignoring them will certainly not make them go away. Therefore, it is wise to address them proactively.

Some of the risks we all face in the values-driven family project are false teaching, peer pressure, media influence, losing a heart connection with our children, unhealthy (worldly) appetites, and of course physical and emotional harm. All of these risks have the potential to derail the entire project, resulting in failure. It is our job as parents to mitigate the risks and to maximize the potential for success.

Concerning matters of risk, it is up to the discretion of the manager (parent) to determine what is allowable. As we mentioned earlier, not all matters in the home are clearly right and wrong, but rather can be described in a *good, better, best* paradigm: *good* having the most inherent risk and *best* having the least risk; obviously decisions are to be made considering both the risks *and* the potential benefits. Yet, since this section is about risk management, we will primarily focus on the risks, not the benefits.

Parenting presents many opportunities for decision-making, and each decision has a different level of risk associated with it. In the risk planning stage, you will want to become aware of these potential pitfalls and choose one of three courses of action: to *mitigate* the risk (take the necessary steps to alleviate difficulty), *avoid* the risk (by making a safer choice) or *accept* the risk (realizing the possible outcomes associated with your choice and moving ahead with the decision). If you decide to accept a higher level of risk, you will want to identify any "triggers" that will signal the presence of a risk factor, and you will determine an appropriate response to minimize the effects. The bottom line in risk management: be aware of the risks and do what is needed to ensure the quality of the outcome that you desire.

Once you have evaluated the risks and made your best decision, the planning phase of risk management is complete; during *execution* (or, living out the plan) we focus on risk control. Risk control involves monitoring for triggers and responding as needed to each situation.

Minimizing the Risks: A Biblical Calling for Parents

Parenting is a unique and challenging responsibility because it demands a balance between *protecting* our children and *preparing* them for the world and for ministering to its lost. Even as adults, there are many areas in which we must exercise caution—and more so for our children, who are emotionally, physically, intellectually, and spiritually more vulnerable and, therefore, more in need of support and nurture.

It is the father's responsibility to protect his children, although both parents will play a part in accomplishing this goal. Jesus used the analogy of a shepherd and his sheep to remind us that there are strangers (thieves and robbers) who will try to enter into the sheep pen, but the shepherd enters by the gate and the sheep listen to his voice because he tenderly leads them. Jesus warned against the "hired hand" who cares nothing for the sheep and will abandon them when he sees the wolf coming. As a result, the flock is scattered (see John 10:1-14).

Though Jesus, in this parable, was speaking of himself as the shepherd of the church, we can see that the father is in a similar role because he is the head of the household and a shepherd of his own flock—his family. We can imagine the father as a protector (or shepherd) of his children. As such, Jesus' story can serve as a caution for us fathers about the importance of keeping our children safe, particularly in regard to spiritual matters, because in this area our children are as defenseless as sheep. We must be aware of the risks associated with passing our children off to the "hired hand" who does not have our child's best interest in mind; such a person does not have a parent's love for the children and will not ensure that they are adequately protected.

External Authorities

There are obviously many benefits to our children's participation in organized group activities and in spending time with external authorities, such as grandparents. Sports, karate, cub scouts, children's church, youth group, dance or music lessons—or any number of wholesome activities—can be a means by which we can teach our children many valuable life skills and nurture beneficial relationships. In our emphasis on risk management, however, we will not deal so much with the advantages of these activities, since for the most part they are readily apparent and will vary based on individual circumstances. Instead, we will focus more on the risks, since this is a not-so-obvious element of decision-making for many.

The risks associated with authorities outside the home are relevant to many of the choices we will make, so this is a good starting point for discussion. An external authority is anyone under whose direction we place our children; this person is the "hired hand" described in the earlier passage. The risk of subjecting our children to an external authority is that this person will not have our loving concern for our child; they may have divided interests; or, they may not be in agreement with our values and what we are teaching our children. To the extreme, we must also protect our children from sexual, physical, or emotional abuse. We like to think that these things will not happen to our children, yet they are all too common—even among family members, friends, and members of the church.

Placing our children under external authorities may weaken our parent/child relationship, jeopardizing the long-term success of the family journey—the goal of which is to emancipate children who are committed to serving God. If our children have stronger bonds with others than with us, they will be less likely to grow into a shared faith (see, for example, Malachi 4:6, Luke 1:17). The effect is akin to the scattering of the flock described in the analogy above (see John 10:12-13).

Likewise, although it is healthy for us, as adults, to question our faith and allow God to strengthen it by answering those questions, external authority figures may bring about confusion or discord in our children if they espouse contradictory teachings or value systems. Our children (because they are, after all, *children*) likely will not have the knowledge or strength of faith to refute these differences and stand firm in their convictions, as we would. If we are aware of the possibility and can be there to discuss these instances with our children and confirm the value and truth of God's precepts, the outcome will be beneficial; yet, if our children do not have this support, they may ultimately wander from the faith.

This is not to say that we should always err on the side of caution and limit our children's interactions to the extreme; it simply means that we will allow this understanding of risk to keep us on our toes in mitigating its negative potential. We have to balance the benefits with the risks. If we put our children under another authority, we should be vigilant in monitoring those interactions; we should be aware, as much as possible, of the value systems and teachings to which our children are exposed as a result of these influences; and we should strive to maintain strong bonds of fellowship with our children that will override all other relationships.

Peer Influences and Socialization

Just as external authorities can pose a risk to raising our children for Christ, so can the influence of peers. This is as true in a Christian setting as in a secular environment. 1 Corinthians 15:33 warns us, "Do not be misled: "Bad company corrupts good character." Likewise, the Proverbs caution that peers can try to influence a child away from what is good, but wisdom and a parent's instruction protect him from harm in this area (Proverbs 1:8-19).

When it comes to socialization, a balanced approach is needed—one that will consider the cost and benefit of the various available alternatives. There are many points of view on this topic, but your decision should be based upon God's Word and what is best for your children and your family. This may mean that you choose not to participate in some activities or that you supervise peer interactions more closely than other children's parents. This is not to be avoided, since the essence of holiness is that we *will* make choices that set us apart and keep us walking more closely with God.

We believe that children can be well socialized within the context of family, particularly if there are a number of siblings—and even more so if the siblings are close in age. In the home environment, children learn conversational skills, positive means of interacting, and cooperative work and play in a safe, nurturing, and loving atmosphere.

As children age, however, same-sex peer relationships become more important. If there are two siblings of the same sex within the family who are close in age, they may become great friends, making outside relationships unnecessary. For children without siblings or those with large age gaps between them, it will be particularly necessary to encourage your child in an appropriate peer relationship. Particularly if your child is in public school, extra-curricular activities can be a means by which they will constructively make use of their time and build these beneficial friendships.

Whatever we choose as an avenue for socialization, we can help guard our children against undue risk by being vigilant in encouraging healthy friendships for them, monitoring those relationships, supervising their peer interactions as much as is practicable, and keeping our own relationship with them strong so that we remain a primary influence.

Home schooling allows you the greatest control over these peer interactions, although one of the risks of home schooling in the area of socialization can be isolationism. If you choose home schooling, you may want to explore children's programs or a youth group within your church. Alternatively, you can participate in a co-op or support group.

Regardless of your choices in this area, the most important consideration for you in helping your child to nurture healthy relationships is whether or not the families you interact with are like-minded. If so, many potential risks will be minimized.

Just as elementary-age children thrive on same-sex peer relationships, children will also unavoidably be drawn to the opposite sex during their teen years. Some families discourage this type of interaction all together, while others do not see any risk associated with these relationships and can run into trouble by failing to recognize problem triggers and respond appropriately. Here again, a balanced approach is best. Certainly, the worldly philosophies regarding what is appropriate may differ considerably from the biblical ideal, so in this area it is necessary to exercise godly wisdom.

A Mother's Role

One of the first planning decisions we usually face in parenting is what role Mom will play within the family—whether she will work full or part time to assist in meeting financial needs, or if she will be home full time as a wife, mom, and homemaker. Of course, there are *good, better,* and *best* options and you will make the choice that is necessary to meet your household management objectives; however, it is wise to be aware of potential risks and plan accordingly.

If both husband and wife feel that Mom's financial contribution is necessary, a *good* option would be for Mom to work part time, if possible, and find suitable care for the children during the hours she must work. There is the most risk associated with this choice, since it would involve outside care for the children and subject Mom to an employer whose influence or decisions could cause difficulty at home.

Again, if income generation is an issue, a *better* option would be for Mom to work from home with a flexible job and schedule so that she can accommodate both work and homemaking responsibilities. A perfect example of this would be the Proverbs 31 woman, who clearly profited for her household by buying and selling (see Proverbs 31:16-18). One of the risks to be considered is that Mom's time and attention would be divided between her work and home responsibilities, which may require some undesirable sacrifices on the home front.

The *best* option, however, would be for Mom to remain at home full time. The Bible says that young women should be encouraged by the older women "to be busy at home" (Titus 2:5). There are many benefits associated with this choice; particularly, eliminating the "hired hand" (a substitute child care provider) and the associated peer group environment and nurturing, instead, the parent-child relationship. It also allows Mom to devote her undivided attention to home management, which is certainly a full-time responsibility. This is a choice with comparatively few risks.

Mom's role in the home is an unavoidable choice that must be made. It is important to consider all of your available options in light of risk management, and plan appropriately to minimize any negative effects on the family.

Day Care

If your family is in a position where Mom needs to work full or part time outside the home, day care will probably be a forced choice. Here again, there are several options, which all have inherent levels of risk.

In terms of risk management, a *good* choice (with the most associated risk) is a licensed day care center. There are benefits to this arrangement, to be sure, but some risks to consider in this environment include: larger group sizes and the resulting risk of peer group interactions that you cannot personally supervise, more frequent childhood illnesses, and, potentially, unknown caregivers.

Likely a *better* choice will be a family day care. This is a more family-oriented environment with smaller group sizes, which can minimize the risk associated with peer group settings. Though there is still a level of risk because the caregiver is not Mom or Dad, a family day care will have a consistent care provider whom you will probably get to know better than those in a more formal day care setting.

Finding family care (a close relative, such as a grandparent or aunt) for your child is, in all probability, the *best* choice, having the least amount of risk. A family care provider is assumed to have a more loving concern for your child and there will probably be more agreement in matters of training, values, etc. It is also probable that peer groups will be non-existent (or greatly minimized) in this setting.

Although we've made certain recommendations for *good, better,* and *best* in regard to child care, these are made with the assumption that all variables are equal. However, a family day care provider or family member is not supervised as is a worker in a licensed day care center. Therefore, if these options present any element of risk for any type of abuse, a day care center may actually be the *best* choice of the three.

As with all of life's decisions, you must go with the alternative that is most in line with the circumstances, needs and goals of your family—what is *best* for you.

School

An education is necessary for children—it is one way of ensuring that they become adults who are capable of interacting in the world, particularly in their ability to make a living. Parents can send their children to public school or private school, or can choose to home school. Certainly, each one has some benefits associated with it, but we'll focus mainly on the risk factors.

It is *good* for parents to faithfully instruct their children in the Lord, which includes reading the Bible, praying, and going to church as a family. This may be accomplished while still sending your children to public school and/or day care. In this scenario, parents can offer a great deal of positive influence to counter-balance the potential negative influences associated with public school.

In using public schools, parents are likely to face more challenges, which can be minimized by making an alternate choice; however, public school is a reality for many families. Some risk factors that will need to be monitored with this choice include: negative peer group interactions, inadequate supervision (particularly at lunch and recess times and bus rides to and from school), unknown authority figures, and curriculum choices and teachings that may deviate significantly from your own values and beliefs. It is wise to consider these various risks and manage them accordingly, particularly if you note a "trigger" that indicates a problem.

An example of a "trigger" and a response may be fitting here, to help you in your own risk management planning. If you have chosen public school and want to mitigate the risks associated with this option, you will be monitoring for problems in any of the risk areas. One trigger that can signal a problem is your child coming home with a permission slip, asking for your consent to administer a particular curriculum for sex education. Your convictions may dictate that your child is too young to have this type of teaching, or you may want to introduce this teaching in the home. As such, your response to this trigger will be to mitigate the risk by refusing to sign the permission slip and explaining the reasons for your decision with your child.

In the area of education, private school may be a *better* choice. Although the risks are similar to public school, they are likely not as pronounced. In a private school setting, class sizes are usually smaller, which can reduce the risks of the peer group environment. Likewise, a private school may have curricula that are more in line with your own values. If you choose this option, you will still need to be vigilant in monitoring for risk triggers.

In our opinion, home schooling offers the *best* environment for faithfully shepherding our children. Deuteronomy 6:6-7 tells us to share the Lord's precepts with our children *all the time*—and only home schooling enables parents to do this. Also, negative influences can be more tightly controlled in the home. Parents can better limit and/or supervise peer group settings, media usage, and the like. There are also no external authorities to contend with.

It is not safe to assume, however, that home schooling is "the" solution. It is simply a vehicle that gives parents more flexibility to properly train, instruct, encourage, love, and administer God's precepts to their children. Doing all of *these* things is what will prove effective in the end.

If you are unfamiliar with home schooling, there are many books and resources that can offer a balanced perspective on its many benefits, as well as providing beginning guidance in how to do it. A good first book for us was *A Field Guide to Home Schooling* by Christine Field, and we would also recommend *Home Schooling: the Right Choice* by Christopher Klicka—but, again, there are a number of others.

Although home schooling is an excellent choice for education, there are risks here, too. One of the first that people commonly point to is socialization, or the potential lack thereof; we have already discussed some possible solutions that would mitigate this risk.

Another risk that may be associated with home schooling is in the quality of education; some parents are concerned that they are not degreed or may not be an adequate teacher for their children. There are so many wonderful curricula and materials now available to homeschoolers, however, that this is almost a non-issue. Likewise, there are a number of home school magazines whose mission is to support parents in this very area by providing reviews of curricula and articles on teaching methods, socialization, and the like. Families can also get involved in a home school co-op or support group for additional helps.

Television, Video Games and Entertainment

In modern times, the risks associated with television viewing (particularly excessive use of the medium) are not unknown; however, families commonly fail to take a proactive stand in minimizing these risks to their children.

At its worst, television brings into our homes not only potentially harmful programming, but insidious commercials as well. We can invite the false teacher, the adulterous wife, the sexually immoral, the drunkard, the wicked, the murderer, the slanderer, the foolish, and the idolater into our living rooms, family rooms, and bedrooms every day via television. The potential spiritual effects of this influence should not be ignored (see Matthew 6:22-23).

Though you may filter the content, the medium itself—the constant panning of the cameras and the barrage of sights and sounds—has a detrimental effect on children's attention spans. And typically, while you may sit down to watch one show, it can easily turn into two or three. Video games and high-intensity, battery-operated toys pose equal risks: they are potential time drains and may also have negative effects on attention span and creativity.

In light of the possible risks, it is *good* to monitor and restrict television viewing and video game usage for your children. It may be even *better* to choose one or two programs that you can enjoy together as a family. We would argue that the *best* option is to eliminate TV and video games all together. You can utilize videos or DVDs for entertainment or educational purposes and catch the news or weather via radio, newspaper, or Internet—you'll find that you don't miss much in keeping the TV off. In fact, children and adults alike will be forced to find more creative and productive uses of their time.

Of course, it is wise to be cautious with Internet use as well, due to the immoral content that is all too easily accessible. You may choose to use a guardian-type of software that requires a password for Internet access or use other parental controls. Ideally, you would visually monitor your children if they are using the Internet for educational purposes.

We should also be cognizant of the risks associated with other forms of entertainment, which may include music, movies, or any number of other leisure activities. Vigilance in these areas is important; just because "everyone else" listens to a certain genre of music or watches a certain new movie that is out, doesn't mean that we must—or that it is *best*.

With almost all forms of entertainment, it is important to be aware of the words that are used and the themes that are emphasized—particularly, sexual immorality, violence, rebellion, and the like. You have the authority to supervise (and restrict, as necessary) your children's entertainment intake, though you should do so with an appeal to the values you share and the fellowship you enjoy as parent and child.

To help you in your evaluation of music, movies, and television for your child, you may want to explore *Plugged In*, a Focus on the Family publication that reviews movies, music, and television from a values-based perspective. The online version can be viewed at www.pluggedinonline.com, or subscribe to the print version via www.family.org.

Another not-so obvious risk that can be associated with almost any form of leisure or recreation is, quite simply, the danger of *excess*. Extremes in *any* area can promote idolatry or simply become a time sink—this can be true of sports, use of technology, interest in cars…the list goes on and on. As such, it's important to make sure that in all of their outside interests, our children are modeling themselves after worthy examples and remaining focused on the Lord. We also want to be sure to encourage them to make the best use of their time (Colossians 4:5).

For us, the *best* option has been family entertainment; we try to find diversions and leisure activities that can be enjoyed by many family members together. Consider some things you can do as a family: go fishing, restore a car, build a model train set, read books, tell stories, play board games, bake cookies, play catch—the possibilities are endless! Perhaps the entire family can be there to cheer on a sibling at a ball game, ballet recital, or other event. These moments can offer great times of fellowship for everyone—and family involvement, rather than individual focus, mitigates the risks of "chaos" and disassociation that can accompany these types of extra-curricular activities. No matter what you choose to do as a family, by pursuing healthy entertainment together, you will be building strong relationships and, by default, eliminating the more negative alternatives.

REFLECTIONS

Questions
1. In project management circles, *acceptable risk* is a variable of quality standards. In the home, this means that if your standards are lower, you will likely be accepting a higher level of risk. Are your quality standards consistent with God's standards? If not, what might you do to better minimize risk?

Practical Applications and *Additional Resources:*
In the *No Greater Joy* bi-monthly publication, Michael Pearl authored a five-part series entitled, "Jumping Ship." Each of the articles in the series discusses some of the things that cause Christian children to "jump ship" and abandon the godly teachings and values of their parents—and what parents can do to keep this from happening. We encourage you to read this series in light of risk management. View the entire series on the NGJ archives at www.nogreaterjoy.org or contact the ministry at 1000 Pearl Road, Pleasantville, TN 37033. An expanded version is also available as a paperback book.

For Additional Study:
Read Luke 14:25-35, where Jesus talks about the cost of being a disciple. What does the passage reveal about the importance of "counting the cost," as it relates to risk management?

Chapter 27: From Planning to Execution: *Team Building*

We've had days where Dad goes to work and Mom has a special dinner to prepare, a ton of housework to do (company's coming!) and a ministry project to attend to—so the easiest thing is to set the older children on "autopilot" with some worksheets for school, find a video for the preschoolers, and let the toddlers have a bit of a free-for-all. Yet what Mom thought would be a productive day for her, turns into a day of settling disputes, listening to bickering, and even (on her part) nagging. On days like this, when we're all doing our own thing, the disunity and the lack of structured attention seem to engender selfishness, arguments, and difficulty. The importance of togetherness and belonging becomes clear. Even in the busyness of life, we need to nurture relationships, or we can experience negative effects—particularly if the sense of division is prolonged.

A project, unlike an activity or task, is unique in that it takes more than one individual to complete it successfully—it takes a team. Parenting involves the entire family and everyone in the family suffers if the "project" fails. Therefore, team building is a vital component of the family. The process of team building is where the project shifts from mere planning to the actual doing, which is known as the *execution* phase.

The unity of the team and its continued focus on the goal starts with wise leadership—after all, behind every successful team is a good coach or an effective leader. In the family project, the responsibility for command falls on the parents—specifically, Dad.

Wise Leadership

Solomon asked God for wisdom in governing his people, because success in leadership depends upon it. From the many biblical illustrations related to leadership, we can summarize the vital characteristics of wise leaders. They: seek the Lord's counsel and help (as did Hezekiah, 2 Kings 18-19; David and Solomon, 1 Chronicles 28; and Asa, 2 Chronicles 15), lead by example (1 Chronicles 29:1-9, 1 Peter 5:2-4), delegate tasks as needed (Exodus 18:17-26, Acts 6:2-4), have the heart of a servant (Matthew 20:20-28, John 13:14-17), and take necessary risks (Genesis 12:1-7, Exodus 3 and 4, Joshua 6).

Household leadership is a daunting task. God gave men a "suitable helper" for a reason. Therefore, work the duties of parenthood and household management as a team. The children should be involved in household duties along with their parents, and all family members should strive to maintain positive relationships, from the top down. One way that Dad, as a wise household leader, can show the attitude of a servant is to ensure that the needs and feelings of his family are considered when making decisions that affect them.

Team Building Begins with Marriage

For any institution, unanimity at the top is vital. If the President and the Chief Operations Officer are not of one mind, there will be trouble within that organization. This holds true within the family as well. For this reason, Dad and Mom must have a consistent message and delivery with the children. If not, children will take advantage of the disunity and play one parent against the other. The result: the team will lack focus on the goal and peace, joy, and success will be elusive. Not good!

The solution: attention to the marriage through expressions of *agape*, a little Greek word that you may remember from the chapter on love. There are some very simple, everyday ways that you and your spouse can practice this self-sacrificial devotion, which goes a long way in maintaining unity between the two of you and creating an atmosphere of love that trickles down and spreads out to affect virtually all areas of family life.

Agape expresses itself through mutual respect and submission, forgiveness, and the like, but these things are often issues of the heart. Ultimately, only God himself can work these things in us through Bible study, prayer, and our genuine desire to exhibit Christ-like character. As we wait patiently for God to shape us and show us how better to live out *agape* within the marriage relationship, it is imperative that we cooperate with God by doing our part in the practical things.

Make an effort to maintain a positive thought life towards your spouse (Zechariah 7:10b, Philippians 4:8). This is important because God's Word tells us that our thoughts affect our words (Luke 6:45b). We want to show God's love through positive speech—both *toward* our spouse and *about* them. Speak those things that are encouraging and helpful, and always speak in love (Ephesians 4:29).

During the day-to-day challenges of life, we try to express sympathy and uplift one another with encouraging speech and with the Word. We also are conscious of how we speak *about* one another. By building each other up in the company of others, we show our respect and love for each other and also guard our own hearts against negative meditations and their ill effects on our relationship.

From thought to speech, and then to action! Think also about how you can express God's love toward your spouse in little ways. You can do this *physically* by helping your partner to fulfill the everyday demands on his or her time or by doing something that will meet a very real need (John 13:12-17, James 2:15-16). It is also important to consider one another's *sexual needs* (see 1 Corinthians 7:3-5) and to minister to one another *emotionally* as an expression of *agape* love (Ephesians 4:32). Try to alleviate emotional stress for your spouse by offering to help out with specific acts of service—and when your spouse is upset, try to be sympathetic even if you can't be empathetic. Small gifts or cards "just because" are also a caring gesture, if your budget permits.

Make *time* for conversation and make time for each other. Brief phone calls or emails during the day help with ongoing communication. You may also try, on occasion, giving the children dinner at the kitchen table and setting up dinner plates for you and your husband in the another room (with the TV off, of course).

Finances can be a sensitive area for many couples. For the benefit of your marriage, try to discuss financial matters in a non-emotional, non-threatening way. Giving each other regular progress reports on the checkbook balance, upcoming bills, etc., can be very helpful in avoiding financial stress. Making time for these updates and having all of the necessary information, as well as being willing to put aside emotions and/or accusations, etc., during such discussions certainly expresses *agape*.

Ultimately, *agape* is a love of action: "For God so loved the world that he *gave* his one and only Son, that whoever believes in him shall not perish but have eternal life" (John 3:16, italics added for emphasis). Just as God showed his love tangibly through the gift of his Son, so we should seek to show love by our giving and our doing for our marriage partners. We will find that in so doing, our love will reciprocate and we will experience, more and more, the true love and joy that God intended for the marriage relationship.

Team Building: Eliminating Arguments and Anger

The atmosphere in the home is of utmost importance in maintaining positive inter-relationships at all levels within the family. If there is acceptance, forgiveness, and unconditional love expressed, then family members will more openly communicate their thoughts, feelings, and needs. Strong bonds of fellowship will help to ensure that the children will embrace the training and teachings of their parents; this is particularly important as emancipation nears.

One area of focus in developing a winning atmosphere, for us, was controlled speech. We all know how easy it is to complain to the children when the perpetual bombardment of even little things begins to overwhelm us as parents. How easy, also, to nag rather than proactively train and encourage—or rather, keep our mouths shut. Yet these empty (or negative) words rarely have any other effect other than to create an atmosphere of discouragement.

The Bible concurs that the tongue (specifically, our speech) is potentially the most damaging of all of the members of the body and, as such, is the most difficult to control (James 3:2-10). This is why we are admonished to watch our words carefully (Ephesians 4:29). It is important not only to *refrain* from inappropriate speech (such as quarreling—see 1 Timothy 2:8) but also to *replace it* with thanksgiving that glorifies God (Ephesians 5:4) and edifies others. What does the Word say about how we are to achieve this goal?

First, ***don't start an argument*** (Proverbs 17:14). Sounds simple, but we all know how much self-control it requires! It's especially difficult in the family, where we all know each other's shortcomings and sensitive spots and we are so tempted to push those buttons.

In particular, the Bible cautions about a quarrelsome wife (Proverbs 19:13, Proverbs 21:9, Proverbs 21:19, Proverbs 27:15-16). Especially if she is a homemaker, her heart, speech, and conduct greatly affect the atmosphere of the home on a day-to-day basis. The Bible equally warns a father not to exasperate his children (Ephesians 6:4), which also translates as "do not irritate" your children (AMP) and "don't make your children angry" (NLT); *The Message* paraphrase links this with not coming down too hard on them. Even though actions may speak louder than words, our words certainly influence our relationships.

As such, **if an argument starts, *do what you can to stop it*.** That may just mean that if your spouse makes a comment, you refuse to take the bait (Proverbs 12:16, Proverbs 17:28, Proverbs 19:11, Proverbs 20:3). Then, take the next step and respond in love. Kindness and understanding can help diffuse a situation that is escalating in a negative direction (Proverbs 15:1).

Arguments and strife often occur because we give in to the expression of anger. Although anger is a natural emotion, it must be controlled (Ephesians 4:26a, Proverbs 29:11), for the Scriptures tell us clearly that "man's anger does not bring about the righteous life that God desires" (James 1:20).

Let's face it, though—children seem to always find ways of driving parents crazy. They have the ability to just wear our patience to the breaking point. Parents are extremely susceptible to lashing out at their children when reaching this critical stage. Therefore, we need to redouble our efforts as frustration builds, to ensure that we are not abusing our position of authority or being hurtful.

Before we began to proactively train our children in proper and expected behaviors, and before we were consistently living and teaching all of the core values with balanced training, encouragement, and discipline, we often found ourselves yelling in response to our children's misbehaviors. We were not merely raising our voices to make an emphatic point to the child (which is certainly effective and sometimes necessary); we were acting out of emotion and using our voices to punish in anger. When it is a result of anger, yelling is not acceptable, and in fact it is counterproductive in regard to training a child in righteousness. Parents must collect themselves first and speak appropriately, in love.

For the sake of team building, at those times when we had raised our voices in anger, we made sure to take the time to restore our children's hearts. It is incredibly cleansing (and an excellent example) if we humble ourselves and apologize for any overreaction or loss of control. Clearing the air in this way is in keeping with the biblical instruction of not letting the sun go down on our anger (Ephesians 4:26). It also helped to ensure that our imperfections as parents would not give Satan a foothold in our children's hearts.

Improving the Mood: Dealing with Irritability and Frustration

Has this ever happened in your home?: the baby cried at 4 AM and you couldn't go back to sleep; the dog got sick on the carpet; the toddler who was partially potty trained peed on the floor three times in a row, for the first time in over a week; the older siblings are perpetually whining and arguing. And as for getting any housework done...! As a result, you are barking out commands to "behave" and "be quiet." In response to your irritable orders, the children are in a crabby mood, too. You see that there is no end in sight. Yet, it's only 9:45! You know you're not going to make it through the day.

This is a very slight exaggeration of a true story—this was us one day! I (Marc) was busy working in my office and took it all in. My pregnant wife then went to the grocery store, children in tow. When she got home, she said that the kids exhibited the worst behavior she had ever experienced with them. I, of course (being the sensitive man that I am), responded, "I could have predicted that."

You see, when everyone is worn thin and everybody is in a bad mood (frustrated, tired, or just plain irritable), things do not just change by themselves. In fact, you can expect the tone in the home to go from bad to worse, if left unchecked. After this incident, I talked to my wife, all the while thinking that the situation was somewhat what it feels like when my computer is acting up. It can be painfully slow or some features can simply stop working. So how do I respond (being as patient as I am with computers)? I click faster and harder and get frustrated that things just seem to slow down more—or, ultimately, the computer just seizes. How do I get things back to normal again? Reboot: *Control—Alt—Delete*! Immediately I saw how the concept can also apply to the family.

First, *control* the situation. Recognize that the environment is not healthy and that the team can't continue down this path. In our home, we stop everything and call a REBOOT. Everyone gathers in a room and sits down. I (or Cindy, if I am not there) tell the family that the mood is dismal and must change.

Next, *alter* the path. Ask the family if they want to have a blessed day. Ask them if they feel blessed now. Then tell them that we need to start over and live by the core values so that we can experience the joy, peace, and success God has in store for us that day.

Finally, *delete* the past. All misdeeds are forgiven. Children receive a clean slate for their encouragement charts and full opportunity to get all their marks. Every person (moody adults included) must give every other member of the family hugs and kisses and tell them they are sorry for being crabby or for doing whatever it was they had done to contribute to the mood crisis.

This method is exceptional! It really works. We have done this and have turned the tone 180 degrees in our home. Rebooting is a staple part of maintaining peace and joy in our home. It helps parents and children alike to recognize that peace, joy, and success are a choice. We as a family unit can set a joyful and loving tone in the home. Implementing this method encourages everyone in the family to come on board as a team and choose to take advantage of the new start offered.

This is a great reflection of the grace that God extends to us through Christ, offering a fresh start when we've chosen the wrong path and come to him in repentance. We urge you to try this method in order to reduce the expression of negative emotions that threaten to wreak havoc in your home. The Bible says, "Better a dry crust with peace and quiet than a house full of feasting with strife" (Proverbs 17:1)—this is so true! Little else matters in a home with a negative tone.

Positive Replacement

Controlling negative emotions is important—but as we remove the negative, we have to *replace* it with something more positive. After all, our mouths were made to utter good, not evil. God gave us the ability to communicate—not to harm each other, but to edify (remember James 3:2-12). We are called to exclusively use our mouths for good and for God's purposes: to love, encourage, and build people up (Ephesians 4:29); to speak as if on God's behalf (1 Peter 4:11a); and to honor God (Ephesians 5:4).

Our speech should always be motivated by love (Ephesians 4:15), truthful (also Ephesians 4:15), and for the recipient's benefit (Ephesians 4:29). We may need to share our feelings about an issue of contention or bring a needed rebuke (with the Word, in love—see 2 Timothy 3:16), but we should do our best to make sure that the recipient's heart is prepared to receive the Word so that they will benefit from it.

Working as a Team

Focusing on the atmosphere of the home is paramount to maintaining loving bonds of fellowship between all the members of the family. Another way in which we try to nurture the team approach is through work. Our children are encouraged and trained to assist in household tasks; we've found that children are capable of far more than the average parent thinks. By contributing to the household duties, children learn many valuable lessons, the most important being the core value of diligence. They also feel pride in their contribution to the household and family and more readily appreciate the work of others on their behalf.

In our home, we start children on chores as soon as they can walk and talk. The benefit of starting young is that they are eager for new challenges and are anxious to be trained on the tasks their older siblings and parents are doing. Likewise, the older children appreciate little helpers and often barter for the younger children as their assistants. In this way, the older children learn management and leadership skills, and the younger children receive valuable, hands-on training.

Remember that there is a learning curve for each job—the child should be expected to work alongside an adult or older sibling for a while, then can work alone with an adult closely supervising the job. Finally, the child should be capable of doing his chores independently, with a quality control check as a follow-up. During this stage, a child's work should not be expected to necessarily meet the standards of an adult's, but it should be done to the best of the child's ability and should be considered "passable."

In addition to larger chores, which our children perform in the morning, they are also asked to help with additional, smaller tasks throughout the day, which may include: feeding pets, clean up of toys, helping with meal preparation, cleaning up after meals, assisting with yard chores (which are usually done by Dad later in the day)...or whatever else Mom or Dad may need help with.

When we first trained our children on chores, we had each one doing an independent task; however, we have also teamed them up to tackle jobs together—two children accomplishing two chores during the morning work time. This helps them develop cooperative work skills, although at first they may need a lot of encouragement (either to keep to work rather than play, or to keep from arguing, bossing, and the like).

We keep our dishes in a low cabinet so the children as young as 18 months can help unload the dishwasher; at this age they are also well able to assist with toy clean up after play time. We let them help with sweeping or dusting, even if it is not at all helpful at first. By age three or four, they fold and put away laundry, set the table, make their beds, and clean bathroom sinks and toilets. A four or five year old is capable of vacuuming, sweeping, dusting, and the like. Older children (8 and above) can be trained to do just about anything an adult can do. There is no limit to what a child can accomplish, with patient training and proper motivation.

What about payment or allowance? Personally, we do not pay our children for doing these routine tasks. We all do them because it is part of our family responsibility—we are a team, working together to get necessary jobs done. Special tasks outside of the routine can be used as opportunities for income generation.

Many people ask us how we get the kids to work when they don't want to. We try to be realistic about what they can accomplish and we also tackle chores first thing in the morning, before they get "tired." A rule of thumb that we've adopted (straight from the Bible) is, "If a man will not work, he shall not eat" (2 Thessalonians 3:10). As such, the children do not have breakfast (or lunch...or whatever the next meal or snack is) until they finish their job. We capitalize on the verse that says: "The laborer's appetite works for him; his hunger drives him on" (Proverbs 16:26). In this way, jobs get done with minimal complaint.

The only problem with chores in the morning is when we have time constraints like going to an appointment. If children go to public school this may also present a challenge. In these cases, another approach may be needed. Whatever schedule you decide upon for chores, remember that a child's appetite and drive for play are great motivational tools that you can use to your advantage.

As children mature (pre-teens and teens), it may not be realistic to do daily chores if they are in school all day *and* come home with homework or participate in extra-curricular activities. An extended Saturday chore time may be a good solution in this case, with outings or participation in activities hinging upon the successful completion of household tasks. The Bible appoints six days for labor and one for rest. Saturday is a break from the weekday routine, but not a break from labor.

As a family, we work hard *and* play hard; in the spirit of team building, we make time to engage in enjoyable "play times" together as a family.

As each family member contributes to the positive atmosphere of the home by resolving to communicate and interact in a healthy and loving way, and as adults and children alike work together for the good of the household, a winning team is created. Strong bonds are forged that are sure to weather the inevitable challenges of life—especially as the children near the age of emancipation.

REFLECTIONS

Questions:
1. When you think about all the ways you can show *agape* love to your spouse, and as a result build a better "team" atmosphere in the home, what are your areas of weakness, and how might you grow in these areas?
2. Honestly evaluate the current atmosphere of your home. How controlled are you in speech and in the expression of your emotions? How does this affect the quality of family relationships?

For Additional Study:
There are many potential study points in the areas of anger management and relationship-building. Just one possibility is to meditate upon the various Scriptures that encourage us to properly manage our emotions. Consider Job 15:11-13, Proverbs 14:29-30, Proverbs 30:32-33, 1 Corinthians 13:4-5, and Colossians 3:8.

Part Four: Parenting on Purpose

Chapter 28: Arriving at the Destination: *Closure*

We have come a long way in our study of this great journey, or rather, the family project. We are now nearing the conclusion—emancipation. In this phase, our children will transition from our authority to autonomy, or rather, will now be directly under God's authority. If we have done our planning well and have been consistent with our execution, this phase can be a beautiful time of fellowship and bonding. On the other hand, if we have been deficient or have miscalculated the condition of our children's hearts, this can be a period of great frustration and heartache.

So what are our final duties while we are still exercising parental authority? First and foremost, while our children are young adults still in our care, we want to ensure that they have the skills and maturity necessary to fulfill the requirements of their imminent duties. Young men must be prepared to be husbands and dads while young women are to be prepared to serve in their respective roles. Hopefully, they have received many years now of consistent modeling and teaching so that the need for our counsel will be limited.

We also want to see to it that our children are capable of managing their money independently. They will soon need to pay their own bills and make their own financial decisions. Hopefully, again, our teaching and modeling of these skills throughout their childhood have been sufficient.

As our children prepare to leave our care, we will also serve as career counselors. One of the more practical matters to address is guiding them in what type of work they should seek. Providing sound counsel as they investigate their options is of utmost importance.

Of course, we would want to discourage them from any career path that is in direct conflict with God's Word. It is best not to commit to a career that supports common cultural vices or that promotes sin—but these are few. Presenting various work options in light of the *good, better,* and *best* paradigm can help our children to make a balanced decision in this area.

Here are some considerations that you can share with your children to help guide them in their career choice:

Natural interests and talents: Most likely, they will find much greater satisfaction in doing a job that interests them. Better yet, they will have true passion about something that is in line with God's call for their lives.

Balance of life's demands: Merging, in some way, the four quadrants of life (work, family, ministry, and rest) helps to achieve greater balance, both personally and within the family. Thus, consider work options that help to maximize time and address multiple areas of family life concurrently. Some examples: full-time ministry (which unites *work* and *ministry*), working from home (balancing both *work* and *family*), a job associated with a personal interest (uniting *work* and *rest*), or "the ultimate:" a home-based, full-time ministry that reflects a personal passion (all four quadrants).

Balancing all of the practical concerns of work, the need for income, and personal goals or interests is of utmost importance in choosing the right career.

It is also wise to consider the demands of the job and any potential impact before making a job commitment (this is especially true when they have a family of their own). Some things to think about include commute time, shift work (if sleep schedules, etc. will be affected), safety, and potential stress.

I (Marc) often pondered 1 Thessalonians 4:11-12 and the biblical admonition to "work with your hands," and one day it spoke to me. At a former job as a senior manager for an engineering consulting firm, I found that my mind was constantly full of information. As a result, I was burdened with stress and many wandering thoughts when away from work. I finally realized that God did not intend for us to abuse our brains in a way that would cause interference with our other duties in life: family, ministry, and rest. These areas of life are all vital components for achieving balance. Information overload, stress, and even our personal ambitions can hinder the accomplishment of God's purposes for our lives and can cause harm to our families. It is wise to pursue balance in this area and choose a career wisely, particularly if we are prone to stress or are unable to leave our work "at the office."

Serving God: Some people need the freedom to do what God wants them to do, or to move as the Spirit leads them. If this is the case, self-employment or flexible employment should be sought.

Keeping holy the sabbath: Honoring the sabbath should be a priority. Because the sabbath is both a day of worship and a day of rest, it is wise to choose a job or career that would allow us to honor God's holy day (Exodus 20:8-11). Exceptions are emergency or vital services and ministry (see Matthew 12:11-12 and Mark 3:3-5).

Seek Freedom: 1 Corinthians 7:20-21 says that we should have peace and contentment about being someone else's servant, if God has put us in that position. On the other hand, it also says that we should gain our freedom if we can.

We are slaves to the one who directs our actions. If it's not a supervisor at work, it may be a creditor who says, "You have to work because the payment is due"; either way, we are equally in bondage. In the United States, however, we have opportunities available that can indeed provide "freedom"—freedom from the restrictions associated with traditional employment arrangements, and even freedom from debt.

The flexibility of self-employment offers freedom to serve God unhindered; likewise, such an employment option *can* lead to financial freedom as well. However, God may choose some to serve in a more traditional work environment. God is personal. The Holy Spirit helps us settle these matters in our own hearts so that we can be assured that we are doing his will.

Finally, a vital aspect of sending our children on their way is to give them sound biblical advice concerning what to look for in a mate. Hopefully they will have shown maturity in choosing their friends wisely, according to many of the Scriptures already presented in the chapter on holiness. Much of this wisdom would generally apply to choosing a life-mate, since this person will become their "best friend," so to speak.

A marriage relationship, however, is a lifelong covenant before God, and not a transient or temporary friendship. As such, the Bible does provide additional guidelines for choosing a marriage partner. Most specifically, we are cautioned to not enter into covenant, contract, partnership, or marriage with an unbeliever (2 Corinthians 6:14-18). We've also already mentioned the curse of the quarrelsome wife; young men should be cautioned in this regard when choosing a potential mate.

Though we are to fellowship with other believers, it is important that we not develop close ties with those commonly referred to as "carnal Christians," or those who have professed faith in Christ but still have one foot planted firmly in the world (1 Corinthians 5:9-11, Luke 8:14). We want to guard against bonding with anyone who may lead us into sin and temptation, or even those who simply discourage us from more holy living that is pleasing to God; this is an especially important consideration for our children as they look forward to courtship and marriage.

These are general cautions about things to avoid, yet we should also offer more positive guidance for our children as to what a good mate will look like. Young women will want to look for a young man who loves the Lord, is stable, and is able to provide for his family. He also should understand his leadership role in the home. A potential wife will similarly love the Lord and will understand her role as a helpmate.

Of utmost importance when young people are entertaining marriage is that they have consistent values and are like-minded, particularly concerning Scripture, family expectations, and their respective roles and responsibilities. For this reason, parental involvement in the courting process is highly recommended and, in fact, alluded to in Scripture (see, for example, Genesis 24).

When the time for emancipation nears, you will simply want to make sure you've covered your bases in these vital areas. As the transition occurs, be prepared to staff the "help desk" for your newly-independent adult children. *Mission accomplished!* The journey is complete and you have arrived at your destination.

REFLECTIONS

Questions:
1. How well prepared for adulthood did you feel as an adolescent, and what do you think you can do differently in preparing your children for a lifetime of serving God?

Practical Applications and *Additional Resources:*
To better prepare your son for his responsibilities as a future husband and father, you may want to provide him with resources like *Manager of His Home: Helping Your Wife Succeed As She Manages Your Home* by Steven Maxwell. You may also benefit from reading *Preparing Sons to Provide for a Single-Income Family*, also by Steven Maxwell and available through www.titus2.com. For preparing girls to be good wives, you may wish to read—and have your older daughter read—*Created to be His Help Meet* by Debi Pearl, available at www.nogreaterjoy.org.

For Additional Study:
John the Baptist is just one example of a child who was raised in the ways of the Lord and, as a result, fulfilled a great Kingdom purpose. Read Luke 1:5-25 and 57-80. In order for John to grow into God's calling for his life, his parents had to be obedient to God's Word and also had to make some tough decisions about social interactions and even diet. Risk management planning certainly applied here—but as a result of his parents being faithful in these tough decisions, John matured to a life of serving the Lord and prepared the way for Christ himself.

Part Four: Parenting on Purpose

Chapter 29: The Journey Begins

You've made it to the end, or is it really just the beginning? Reading is easy—applying what you've read is a little more difficult. This is especially true if this is all new to you, or if you're a husband or wife who wants to incorporate some of this into daily life, yet don't have agreement about it with your spouse. If you like the ideas but aren't sure you have what it takes to make the tough decisions that seem to be required for living this "values-driven family" lifestyle, this can seem daunting. Many things can hinder the implementation of new ideas and methods for you and for your family—even if the benefits of doing so seem very attractive.

At this point, applying the concepts outlined in this book may seem overwhelming. We have touched upon the importance of balance in many areas of life—and implementing these ideas is no different.

The most important thing to remember is that God is at the center of it all. He is the Creator of all things. He has a perfect plan for our good that has been worked out throughout all of human history, and will continue to be worked out in and through us.

God wants us to turn to him and acknowledge his reality, his truth, and his goodness. As we grow in our awareness of God and realize just who he is, we realize that he is worthy of our best efforts in living. Living by the values that God values is for his glory, but it's also for our own good. It's a reciprocally beneficial adventure. We bless and honor God when we live in a way that pleases him; in return, he blesses us with joy, peace, success, and many other wonderful things—in addition to the gift of eternal life that is already ours when we put our trust in Jesus.

God is not a cosmic dictator up in heaven giving us a list of rules. Although his Word is clear about what is right and wrong, he gives us boundary conditions that are ultimately for our own good; and as we live within them, we find that there is great liberty. God made each of us unique and, although he has general purposes for us collectively, we each play a special part in his overall plan. He has given us different attributes, experiences, skills, abilities, and passions. He wants us to use all of these things for his glory and to accomplish his plans. As we do so, we find a greater fulfillment than anything else that this world could offer.

If we truly desire God's best and are willing to do *our* best—if we focus on the big picture, which is Christ himself—everything else is just small stuff. All we have to do is seek him, and we will find him. So don't worry about the "doing"—just look to the One who has the power to do it! If the desire of your heart is to live life God's way, he will help you with all of the resources at his mighty hand.

Although we have looked at each of the core values of God individually, we must remember that God is the source of it all, and we must allow him to direct us in the way they are lived out. Living the life that God desires and receiving the benefits thereof means living out *all* of the core values *in concert* to the best of our abilities. We can't pick and choose from the ones that seem easiest or the ones that have the most appeal. We experience *some* benefit from living out *some* of the core values—but the fullness of life and all of its joy is only achieved as we strive to live according to *the whole* of God's Word.

Though this seems impossible, God is patient as he shapes us in greater Christlikeness. We all have blind spots, or areas where we fail to see our deficiencies; if God allows this, it means that we may not be led by the Spirit to address certain shortcomings just yet. If we are sensitive to the Holy Spirit and committed to living a godly life, he will be faithful to show us, one area at a time, what he wants us to work on. So be patient with yourself, be encouraged that God is a good and loving father, and persevere in working out your salvation with fear and trembling (Philippians 2:12).

God has promised us his help in every situation and at all times—remember, it's all about direction, not perfection. God is more concerned with our hearts than with our actions. If we are truly seeking him and his ways, we can expect his abundant love, grace, mercy, and goodness—even at those times when we feel we fall short. And we can equally expect that our actions will fall more and more in line with our heart's desire as we continue to faithfully live out God's precepts.

We have tried to offer many practical applications that can help to set your family life on the path of God's best. Again, remember that you will be taking this step-by-step; it is a process, not an immediate outcome.

You've pressed on to the completion of this book—that means you have a great desire to see your family doing life together in a way that honors God. You want to do your best as a parent in every area of life so that you—and your children—continually experience God's blessing. You want to see your children come to adulthood with all of the worldly skills they need—but also with spiritual strength and godly character.

At this point, we would simply leave you with an encouragement to *begin* this great adventure! Set your eyes on the ultimate goal, be faithful to your call and your duties as parents and servants of the Most High God, and be committed to pursuing God's purposes by living out his precepts. The rewards are too numerous to list—but here are a few: abundant peace and joy, prosperity, honor among men, the esteem of God himself, and the immense feeling of success that comes from having lived out (to the best of your ability) God's perfect plans for your family. God is a rewarder of those who earnestly seek him—so look to him in all you do, remain steadfast in your commitment to progress, praise the Lord at all times, and rejoice in the wonderful things that he will do! Now, go and do *your* part—and God will do *his*.

Values Driven Publishing was established with a mission: to support ministry leaders in their efforts to get Great Commission-oriented works in print and into the hands of the folks who will benefit from them. VDP provides services needed to publish, print, and distribute Christian books. VDP is a full-service publishing house offering a-la-carte publishing, post-production, and marketing services. Visit www.valuesdrivenpublishing.com for more information.

About the Authors

Marc Carrier wears many hats. He is the co-owner of Values-Driven, a ministry and family business committed to equipping folks to make the most of every opportunity. Marc is also an author, evangelist, church leader, missionary, trainer, and speaker at churches and homeschooling events. However, he considers his most important role to be that of husband and father. He takes an active role in both discipling and homeschooling his six children and integrates family into his business and ministry as much as is possible. Marc is likewise passionate about both sharing the Gospel and challenging and inspiring others in their commitment to personal and spiritual growth and service.

Marc is co-author of *The Values-Driven Family*, *Values-Driven Discipleship*, and most recently, *The Values-Driven Life*. The overarching theme and purpose of these works is to challenge and inspire Christians to align their lives with God's precepts and to experience the abundant life that Christ offers, as parents and as followers of Christ. Marc has been featured on the LeSea Network's *The Harvest Show* as well as numerous radio programs, including SRN News, Concerned Women for America, and KLOVE.

Cynthia Carrier is an author and sought after speaker. Her passions include homeschooling, parenting and women's emotional and spiritual wholeness. She received her degree in Elementary Education from the University of Connecticut. She was a preschool teacher and Director before having children of her own. She is now the homeschooling mother of six children (with number seven due shortly).

Cindy has written additional books, including *The Growing Homeschool: Integrating Babies and Toddlers into Your Already Busy Schedule* and *Growing to be Like Jesus: A Color and Learn Activity Book*. Cynthia has also co-authored *Values-Driven Discipleship: Biblical Instruction and Character Training Manual*. Cindy has prepared powerful and encouraging audio seminars entitled *Muddling through Motherhood: Experiencing Joy in the Midst of Occasional Chaos* and *Defeating Depression: Cooperating with God to Experience Victory over Negative Emotions*.

Other Values-Driven Solutions

In ***The Values Driven Life: Accelerated Growth for the Christian Soul*** Marc and co-author Todd Shaw take you on a journey through the character traits that exemplify the essence of Christ-likeness, *the values that God values*. These biblical precepts provide the fertilizer to accelerate your growth as a fruitful follower of Christ and align your life on the center of God's will.

Values Driven Discipleship: Biblical Instruction and Character Training Manual is a perfect companion manual for *The Values Driven Family*, suitable for family devotions, biblical instruction, and leveraging life's teachable moments with your children.

The Growing Homeschool: Integrating Babies and Toddlers into Your Already Busy Schedule will provide wisdom and encouragement to inspire moms to make the most of every opportunity integrating little ones into their homeschool routines

Growing to be Like Jesus is a color and learn activity book centered around the core values presented in the Values-Driven series of books. Your littles will learn biblical character and practical copy work and motor skills.

Muddling through Motherhood: Experiencing Joy in the Midst of Occasional Chaos—The title says it all. Let Cindy, an experienced mom, encourage you to reach for God's best while in the trenches of motherhood.

Defeating Depression: Cooperating with God to Experience Victory Over Negative Emotions—Let Cindy share her testimony and provide biblical insight and encouragement so that you too can experience victory as she has.

Home Management Bundle—Need help with getting organized. Let the Carriers provide some great tools to help you maximize your effectiveness—including intuitive budget software and schedule templates.

BeeYouTiful all-natural health products are sold at a 15% discount at www.valuesdrivenfamily.com.

For many downloadable **FREEBIES**, sign up for our informative e-newsletter.

For insight and encouragement, visit the Carrier family blog at www.valuesdrivenfamily.blogspot.com.

For these products, visit **www.valuesdrivenfamily.com**.

Printed in the United States
150748LV00003B/1/P